Contents

Section 1: Rules of Engagement

Section 2: Boot Camp

Section 3: Battlefields

FIGHTING FOR THE

Soul

OF YOUR CHILD

A PRACTICAL GUIDE TO BIBLICAL PARENTING

LEARNING COMPANION

FIGHTING
FOR THE

Soul

OF YOUR
CHILD

**A PRACTICAL GUIDE TO
BIBLICAL PARENTING**

JIMMY & KAREN EVANS
JULIE EVANS ALBRACHT

XO
PUBLISHING

XO MARRIAGE™

Fighting for the Soul of Your Child: Learning Companion
Copyright © 2024 by Jimmy Evans, Karen Evans, and Julie Evans Albracht

Unless otherwise noted, Scripture taken from the New King James Version®. Copyright © 1982 by Thomas Nelson. Used by permission. All rights reserved.

Scripture quotations marked (NASB) are taken from the (NASB®) New American Standard Bible®, copyright © 1960, 1971, 1977, 1995, 2020 by The Lockman Foundation. Used by permission. All rights reserved. Lockman.org.

Scripture quotations marked (NLT) are taken from the *Holy Bible*, New Living Translation, copyright © 1996, 2004, 2015 by Tyndale House Foundation. Used by permission of Tyndale House Publishers, Carol Stream, Illinois 60188. All rights reserved.

Scripture quotations marked (NIV) are taken from the Holy Bible, New International Version®, NIV®. Copyright © 1973, 1978, 1984, 2011 by Biblica, Inc.™ Used by permission of Zondervan. All rights reserved worldwide. www.zondervan.com. The "NIV" and "New International Version" are trademarks registered in the United States Patent and Trademark Office by Biblica, Inc.™

All rights reserved. No portion of this publication may be reproduced, stored in a retrieval system, or transmitted in any form by any means—electronic, mechanical, photocopying, recording, or any other—without prior permission from the publisher. "XO Marriage" is a trademark registered in the United States Patent and Trademark Office by XO Marriage.

ISBN: 978-1-960870-28-5

XO Publishing is a leading creator of relationship-based resources. We focus primarily on marriage-related content for churches, small group curriculum, and people looking for timeless truths about relationships and overall marital health. For more information on other resources from XO Publishing, visit XOMarriage.com.

XO Marriage™, an imprint of XO Publishing
1021 Grace Lane
Southlake, TX 76092

While the authors make every effort to provide accurate URLs at the time of printing for external or third-party Internet websites, neither they nor the publisher assume any responsibility for changes or errors made after publication.

Printed in the United States of America

24 25 26 27—5 4 3 2 1

Meet the Authors

JIMMY & KAREN EVANS founded MarriageToday (now called XO Marriage) in 1994 to help couples thrive in strong and fulfilling marriages. Together, they hosted *MarriageToday with Jimmy and Karen*, a television show and ministry designed to bring hope and healing to hurting couples. Jimmy has written more than 50 books including *Marriage on the Rock*, *The Four Laws of Love*, *21 Day Inner Healing Journey*, and *Tipping Point*. Karen is the author of *From Pain to Paradise*. Jimmy and Karen have been married for more than 50 years, and they are coauthors of *Fighting for the Soul of Your Child* and *Vision Retreat*. They have two married children and five grandchildren.

JULIE EVANS ALBRACHT is the daughter of Jimmy and Karen Evans. She and her husband, Cory, have been married almost 30 years and have adult twin daughters named Elle and Abby. This is Julie's second book to work on with her father. Julie had the concept idea for *Where Are the Missing People?*, a post-Rapture guide for those left behind. Jimmy and Julie also had a podcast called *Standing for Truth*. Julie is a coauthor of *Fighting for the Soul of Your Child.* She and Cory reside in the Texas Hill Country where Julie lives out her love and passion as an interior designer, alongside her desire to share a life lived from a biblical perspective.

Dear Friends

Raising godly children is both an incredible privilege and a profound responsibility, especially in a world that challenges biblical values. A spiritual battle rages for the souls of our children, and as parents, it is our duty to stand up and fight.

Fighting for the Soul of Your Child: Learning Companion is complementary to our book *Fighting for the Soul of Your Child*, and it serves three purposes:

1. To deepen parents' understanding of the book's key principles;

2. To facilitate meaningful conversations in both group and family settings;

3. To encourage self-reflection and personal application.

We designed *Learning Companion* to be adaptable for both group study and personal reflection.

If you're part of a group, the discussion questions will provide an opportunity to engage in thought-provoking conversations with other parents. Meanwhile, for individuals, the personal reflection questions will lend to eye-opening introspection and self-discovery.

Whether you're contemplating parenthood, grappling with rebellious children, or navigating the cultural challenges impacting your kids, *Learning Companion* provides truth, wisdom, and practical support. While we don't claim to possess all the answers, we firmly believe that God's Word is sufficient for any situation we encounter.

You don't have to be a perfect parent to participate. We all make mistakes along our parenting journeys. Thankfully, we have a loving heavenly Father who lifts us up when we fall. We are confident that He will use this guide to strengthen, encourage, and prepare parents as we seek Him together and fight for the spiritual well-being of our children.

In a world where traditional values and the sanctity of life are under attack, we must stand firm in defending our beliefs. Remember the words of the apostle Paul: "For we do not wrestle against flesh and blood, but against principalities, against powers, against the rulers of the darkness of this age, against spiritual hosts of wickedness in the heavenly places" (Ephesians 6:12). We're not fighting against people who disagree with us but rather with an antichrist spirit that seeks to steal, kill, and destroy. Our children are precious gifts, and it's our responsibility to raise them to love and serve the Lord.

We look forward to diving into God's Word and wisdom with you! Let's commit to showing up with open hearts and minds, ready to learn and grow together. God has incredible things in store for our families as we partner with Him in parenting.

With gratitude and anticipation,
Jimmy and Karen Evans
Julie Evans Albracht

How to Use Learning Companion

The chapters in this book directly parallel the chapters in *Fighting for the Soul of Your Child*.

Recap

Beginning with Session 2, the recap is a concise summary of the key points discussed in the previous chapter. (Session 1 does not include a recap.)

The Big Idea

The Big Idea is the primary theme, idea, or principle of the chapter.

Chapter Review

We review the chapter and highlight important insights and details.

Key Scriptures

We share several key verses or passages that relate to the chapter's content.

Discussion Questions

Thought-provoking questions guide readers to engage in meaningful conversations with others, whether in a group or family setting.

Personal Reflection Questions

Introspective questions encourage self-reflection as they deepen understanding and personal application of the material.

Connect with the Father

Sample prayers help you bring what you've learned to the Lord in prayer, as you ask the Holy Spirit to guide you into His truth.

Until Next Time …

If possible, read the next chapter in *Fighting for the Soul of Your Child.* Though *Learning Companion* covers the key principles, we believe reading the full chapter will help you have increased clarity and greater insight into the material. Always ask the Lord, "What do You want me to learn from this chapter?"

Leaders

We are deeply honored to welcome the men and women who will lead groups through *Fighting for the Soul of Your Child: Learning Companion.* Your willingness to give of your time, effort, and energy is a testament to your love for the Lord and for families. The desire of our hearts is to equip and empower parents with the biblical wisdom and practical tools necessary to navigate the complexities of godly parenting in today's ungodly world.

Leaders, you will have the incredible opportunity to facilitate life-changing conversations and provide support to parents who are seeking God's guidance in raising their children. On the following pages we have included a sample session schedule with details for each part of the session, as well as some words of wisdom. We highly encourage you to obtain your own copy of *Fighting for the Soul of Your Child* so that you can review the chapters in depth. We pray that as you read, the Lord will highlight key

Scriptures and principles that will minister specifically to the people in your group.

Remember, you are not alone in this endeavor. We are praying for you and believing that God will use you mightily and make a lasting difference in the lives of every family in your group.

Thank you once again for your commitment. We look forward to the wonderful journey ahead and the incredible transformation that will take place in the lives of parents and children alike through your leadership.

May God bless you abundantly as you serve Him and His people.

Sample Session Schedule

Opening Prayer: 2 Minutes

This brief prayer sets the tone and expectation for the session. The following is an example:

> *Dear Father, thank You for bringing this group together. We believe that You have given us the incredible privilege of fighting for our children, and we ask You, Holy Spirit, to open our hearts to receive whatever You have for us today. In Jesus' name, Amen.*

Engage and Recap: 5 Minutes

For the first session, focus on engagement by introducing each member or couple, going over the schedule, and sharing intended goals for the group.

For the subsequent sessions, briefly engage and then recap the previous week's chapter(s).

Read: 20 Minutes

Read aloud the chapter review and key Scriptures for the chapter(s) you will be discussing. For the first session, we recommend that you as the leader do the reading. Then in subsequent session, you can invite a group member to read. It is best to ask them privately beforehand to ensure they are comfortable doing so.

Talk: 20 Minutes

Ask one discussion question at a time and invite the group members to answer. Do not rush.

It may take a few moments for someone to volunteer to talk, and that is okay. When a group member does answer, show genuine interest in what they are saying. As the leader, you have the delicate responsibility to ensure everyone has an opportunity to share their thoughts and feelings without any individual dominating the conversation.

- If time is short, select one or two discussion questions to focus on during the Talk time.

- Personal reflection questions are intended to be answered privately or with one's spouse following the session.

Group Prayer ("Connect with the Father"): 10 Minutes

The sample prayers are intended to be a starting point. If time permits, you may wish to begin by asking the group for any prayer requests. This is an opportunity to show God's love and grace as you will likely hear a wide array of needs, concerns, and stories. This is not the moment for teaching or correction; instead, bring all the prayers to the Lord, asking for His wisdom and guidance. If you feel it is imperative to follow-up on any particular request, have that conversation privately after the session.

Closing (Until Next Time): 3 Minutes

Tell the group what chapter(s) they should read in *Fighting for the Soul of Your Child* before the next session. Remind them to ask the Lord, "What do You want me to learn from this chapter?"

Words of Wisdom

Prepare with Prayer

Begin each session with prayer, seeking God's guidance and wisdom for the group. Pray for the parents and their families, asking for insight into their specific needs.

Plan Ahead

Read the chapter(s) from *Fighting for the Soul of Your Child* that you will be addressing during the upcoming session. Review any specific Scriptures and questions that you want to highlight.

Create a Welcoming Environment

The sessions should have an atmosphere of trust and respect in which parents can comfortably and confidentially share their concerns and challenges without fear of judgment. Remember, no one has perfect kids, and no parent is perfect either. We are all in this fight together!

Encourage Participation

Actively involve all group members by asking open-ended questions and inviting everyone to share their insights and personal stories. No individual should be allowed to monopolize the conversation, and even though you are the leader, resist the urge to dominate the discussion.

Actively Listen

When a group member speaks, show genuine interest in what they have to say through your eye contact and body language. Ask follow-up questions to deepen the conversation.

Be Flexible

Be open to the leading of the Holy Spirit during your meetings. Sometimes the most profound moments happen spontaneously. Adapt to the needs of your group as they arise.

Respect Differences

Understand that other parents may have different parenting styles and experiences. Respect these differences and encourage open dialogue, always pointing back to the foundational truth of God's Word.

Be Consistent

Follow the schedule you establish at the first session. This helps parents plan and prioritize participation.

Lead by Example

If possible, silence your cell phone and remove any other distractions. When you are fully present and engaged, you demonstrate the same commitment to the session that you would like to see from the group members. Both within and outside the group, ensure your words, actions, and attitudes reflect your love for Jesus and others.

Section 1

RULES OF ENGAGEMENT

The Greater Purpose

The Big Idea

Your greater purpose as a parent is to teach and train your child to know and love God.

Chapter Review

The Bible holds the answers to life's biggest questions, and parenting is no exception. But before we look at the purpose of parenting, we need to look at what the Bible says about the purpose of every individual. According to Deuteronomy 6:4–5 and Matthew 22:35–38, our purpose is to love God. An essential part of loving God is knowing Him, because you can't really love someone you don't know. Therefore, to love God, you have to know the real Him and spend time with Him on a daily basis.

You can only get as close to God as your concept of Him will allow. Here are three things every person needs to know:

- **God is a good God.** Most of us develop our first concepts of God from our parents as we grow up. It's great if children have generous, loving, and kind parents, but if they have distant, uncaring, legalistic, or abusive parents, then they tend to think of God in those terms. God is good and *only* good. He always keeps His promises, He always provides, and He has never once turned His back on anyone.

- **God is loving.** *Agape* is the only expression of love that doesn't require an emotion. Yes, God has emotions, but His love doesn't require them, because He *is* love. When Jesus tells us to love our neighbors as ourselves in Mark 12:31, this is *agape*. We choose to love them the same way God chooses to love us.

- **God is gracious.** The Lord is good, even when you don't deserve His goodness. He loves you even when everyone else thinks you're unlovable. Every person deserves God's wrath, but Jesus took your place on the cross *and* the punishment for your sins. If you receive Him by faith, the curse of sin is forever removed from your life.

Now, let's look at what the Bible says about your purpose as a parent. According to Deuteronomy 11:18–21; Proverbs 22:6; and Ephesians 6:4, **your greater purpose as a parent is to teach and train your child to know and love God**. This is your mission, your chief assignment. Teaching and training are often used interchangeably, but there is an important distinction. In Deuteronomy 11, parents are told to teach their children God's commands by "speaking of them" four specific times: when you are at home, when you are traveling, when you are going to bed, and when you wake up in the morning. In Proverbs 22:6, the word "train" comes from the Hebrew word *chanak*, which means 'to put something into the mouth.' Pulpit Commentary offers this picture: "To give to be tasted as nurses give to infants food that they have masticated in order to prepare it for their nurslings."[1] An adult would pre-chew the food and then put it in the infant's mouth, thus demonstrating the way to eat. When you train a child, you aren't simply talking. Yes, you are telling them something, but you are also living that something in front of them.

There is a divine *why* behind everything you do. Parents are the image-bearers of God to their children and the filter by which their children view God. Do you want to your child to know and love God because of your behavior or in spite of it? We must remember that God is the Creator of the family. Therefore, only His purpose will empower us to raise our children properly. Parenting takes tremendous faith, commitment, and patience. It is not a spectator sport. In fact, it's not a sport at all. It's real life, with eternal life-and-death consequences. We don't say this to scare you but to encourage you to take it seriously. No one can successfully parent alone. We all need God's help.

Key Scriptures

Hear, O Israel: The LORD our God, the LORD *is* one! You shall love the LORD your God with all your heart, with all your soul, and with all your strength (Deuteronomy 6:4–5).

Then one of them, a lawyer, asked *Him a question*, testing Him, and saying, "Teacher, which *is* the great commandment in the law?"

Jesus said to him, "'You shall love the Lord your God with all your heart, with all your soul, and with all your mind.' This is *the* first and great commandment" (Matthew 22:35–38).

Therefore you shall lay up these words of mine in your heart and in your soul, and bind them as a sign on your hand, and they shall be as frontlets between your eyes. You shall teach them to your children, speaking of them when you sit in your house, when you walk by the way, when you lie down, and when you rise up. And you shall write them on the doorposts of your house and on your gates, that your days and the days of your children may be multiplied in the land of which the LORD swore to your fathers to give them, like the days of the heavens above the earth (Deuteronomy 11:18–21).

And you, fathers, do not provoke your children to wrath, but bring them up in the training and admonition of the Lord (Ephesians 6:4).

Train up a child in the way he should go,
And when he is old he will not depart from it
(Proverbs 22:6).

Discussion Questions

1. Before reading this chapter, what was your view on the purpose of parenting? How did cultural, social, or personal factors influence your view?

2. How do you balance the desire for your children to be happy and successful with the recognition that they will face challenges and failures in life?

3. What is the difference between teaching and training, and why are both important for your children?

4. What are some practical ways you can seek God's guidance and support in fulfilling your role as a parent?

Reflection Questions

1. How did your parents or guardians influence your understanding of God and your purpose in life? How has this influenced your approach to parenting?

2. How do you strive to reflect God's character in your interactions with your children?

3. Parenting is a divine mission with eternal consequences. How does this perspective change the way you view the challenges and joys of raising children?

Connect with the Father

Dear Father, we need Your wisdom and guidance on this journey of parenthood. Your Word teaches us that our ultimate purpose is to love and know You with everything that we are, and as parents, we are to teach and train our children to do the same. Show us how to instill a deep, lasting love for You in our children's hearts as we partner with You to meet their needs. Holy Spirit, help us to raise our children with intention and grace, knowing that our actions and behaviors shape their understanding of You. In Jesus' name, Amen.

Until Next Time …

- Read Chapter 2: Basic Training.
- Ask the Lord, "What do You want me to learn from this chapter?"

Chapter 2 Guide

Basic Training

Recap

- Our purpose is to love God, who is good, loving, and gracious.

- Your purpose as a parent is to teach and train your child to know and love God.

- Parents are the image-bearers of God to their children and the filter by which their children view God.

- No one can successfully parent alone. We all need God's help.

The Big Idea

When a child is grown and ready to leave home, the parents should be able to say two things:

1. "We have done everything we could to teach and train our child to know and love God."

2. "We have met every major need in our child's life in a faithful and sacrificial manner."

Chapter Review

Parents must understand the four fundamental needs of a child that only God can completely satisfy: identity, security, purpose, and acceptance. A child's perception of God and their understanding of His nature are profoundly shaped by their parents' character and treatment of them. Parents who embody love and truth while actively participating in their child's development pave the way for the child to know and love the Lord. But when parents are absent, cruel, or abusive, their children's needs go unmet, making it harder for the children to establish a relationship with God.

Parenting is more about setting an example than teaching through words. Children are significantly influenced by their parents' actions, attitudes, language, friends, church involvement, and the quality of their marriage. Attempting to impose religious beliefs on a child without living out those beliefs is ineffective and doesn't provide the necessary role model.

The twofold purpose of each parent is to

1. Teach and train a child to know and love God.

2. Meet the four basic needs of the child.

Need #1: Acceptance

Acceptance is fundamental for a child's sense of self-worth and belonging. Parents must demonstrate love and acceptance from birth onward through four key methods:

1. Physical Affection

The human need for physical affection is profound and extends across a lifetime. However, it is during childhood that this need is particularly critical, profoundly impacting physical, social, and emotional development. Research highlights the fact that touch activates various brain systems essential for optimal physiological development.

The less parents touch and hold their children, the more emotionally detached and rejected the children are likely to feel. I (Jimmy) had a father who didn't touch me from the time I was three years old until I was 38 years. That's a 35-year gap! My mother wasn't very affectionate either. The absence of physical touch, referred to as "touch deprivation" or "skin hunger," increases feelings of loneliness, anxiety, and depression. It triggers the production of the stress hormone cortisol, leading to increased heart rate, blood pressure, respiration rate, and muscle tension.

2. Verbal Affirmation

Children need to hear "I love you" every day, and they also need to be praised and complimented throughout their lives. An atmosphere of verbal affirmation builds strong parent-child bonds and fosters self-belief.

3. Availability

Children need both quality time and large quantities of time with their parents, especially in their early years. Children spell love "t-i-m-e." Parents who prioritize other activities at the expense of spending time with their children leave them feeling neglected and unimportant.

4. Expression

Every child needs a sense of belonging and a sense of identity and individual expression. A healthy person always has a balanced sense of who they are and to whom they belong. An unhealthy person either feels a lack of belonging or a lack of identity. Parents who try to over-control a child's life or make that child into something they want them to be are harming the child. Yes, parents should lead a child in the right direction, but they also should give the child room to be an individual and to make certain personal choices.

Need #2: Identity

All of us have a deep need to feel unique and significant. Parents communicate this sense of identity to their children by letting them know how special they are. A child should not be compared to brothers or sisters or made to overly conform to the family system. Rather, a child should be allowed to express themself in an atmosphere of love and order. The older children get, the more their feelings and opinions should dictate the direction of their lives. Children should not be given the freedom to self-destruct, but they should have the right to be who God made them to be and to find themselves within safe parameters and in His will.

Need #3: Security

A child's sense of security mainly depends on how stable their parents' lives are. When children see tension at home, they start feeling uneasy, but they feel secure when they see their parents love and serve each other. Children feel loved when they are raised with a balance of accountability and acceptance. Parents must institute rules and boundaries and hold their children accountable for disobedience.

Need #4: Purpose

Young children need to be taught that God has a special purpose for their life that will be revealed someday. Parents should give children increasing responsibilities around the house while also making sure they have time to be children and play. Children should be involved in church and the community as they learn how to use their spiritual gifts to serve others. Children are happier when they feel like they have a purpose.

Society has all kinds of opinions about raising children, and we have to be diligent to find out what God's Word says and then follow it.

Scripture Reading

My God will meet all your needs according to the riches of his glory in Christ Jesus (Philippians 4:19 NIV).

Seek first the kingdom of God and His righteousness, and all these things shall be added to you (Matthew 6:33).

Delight yourself also in the LORD,
And He shall give you the desires of your heart (Psalm 37:4).

The Lord is my shepherd;
I have all that I need (Psalm 23:1 NLT).

Discussion Questions

1. Why is modeling God's character and love more important than just telling kids what to do? How can you align your actions with your values?

2. How can parents make sure their kids feel unconditionally accepted while still providing accountability?

3. How can parents give kids a sense of identity and purpose without forcing unrealistic expectations on them? Where is the balance?

4. How can parents create a secure home environment even in the midst of life's chaos and struggles? What boundaries and habits help?

Reflection Questions

1. How were your needs for acceptance, identity, security, and purpose met or not met by your parents? How did this impact your view of yourself and God?

2. Since parenting is more caught than taught, what are your children "catching" from you?

3. What habits or attitudes do you need to change to better reflect God's love to your kids?

4. How are you seeking God's wisdom and strength to parent with purpose? What support do you need most right now in this challenging job?

Connect with the Father

Dear Father, help us to nurture our children's sense of identity and allow them to express the uniqueness You have given them. Give us strength as we work hard to provide a secure and stable home, free from strife and discord, where they can grow in their relationship with You. Teach us how to balance love and truth as we invest ourselves faithfully in their development. Guard our tongues from harshness and shame, so our children always feel Your unconditional love through us. May our actions and words always reflect Your character. In Jesus' name, Amen.

Until Next Time …

- Read Chapter 3: The Soul War.
- Ask the Lord, "What do You want me to learn from this chapter?"

Chapter 3 Guide

The Soul War

Recap

- The twofold purpose of each parent is to teach and train a child to know and love God and to meet the four basic needs of the child (affection, identity, security, and purpose).

- Parents demonstrate acceptance through physical affection, verbal affirmation, availability, and expression.

- Children develop their identity and sense of security through their parents.

- Children are happier when they feel like they have a purpose.

The Big Idea

We are to love the Lord with our soul—everything we are and have—and teach and train our children to do the same.

Chapter Review

The concept of *soul* (from the Old English *sāwol*) can be found all the way back in Genesis. On the sixth day of creation, "the LORD God formed man of the dust of the ground, and breathed into his nostrils the breath of life; and man became a living **soul**" (Genesis 2:7 KJV, bold added). Now, Genesis was written in Hebrew, and the Hebrew word for soul is *nephesh* (pronounced neh'-fesh). Man was just a dust-made body at first, but with God's breath, he became a *nephesh*. According to Strong's Concordance, *nephesh* can be defined as "living being, life, self, person" but also "desire, passion, appetite, [and] emotion."[1]

Nephesh appears 754 times in the Old Testament, and it is often used to describe a person's essence—the very fiber of their being. The restoration of your soul is the restoration of your very self. To long for the Lord's courts is to long with all your passion. And to be joyful in God is to rejoice with all your emotion.

The Greek equivalent of *nephesh* is *psuché* (pronounced psoo-khay'). It literally means 'breath' and is used to denote "the vital force," "that in which there is life," and "the seat of the feelings, desires, affections, [and] aversions."[2] *Psuché* can also be transliterated as *psyche*, and this is the root of our English word psychology (literally "the study of the soul").

In the first chapter, we examined two Scriptures that outline our purpose as humans. Let's look at those again, this time in light of the full meaning of *nephesh* and *psuché*:

> Hear, O Israel: The LORD our God, the LORD *is* one! You shall love the LORD your God with all your heart, with all your soul [*nephesh*], and with all your strength (Deuteronomy 6:4–5).

> Jesus replied, "The most important commandment is this: 'Listen, O Israel! The LORD our God is the one and only LORD. And you must love the LORD your God with all your heart, all your soul [*psuché*], all your mind, and all your strength'" (Mark 12:29–30 NLT).

Loving the Lord with all your *nephesh* and *psuché* means loving Him with everything you have and holding nothing back. You cannot deny Him any portion of your being. Every part of your self—your desires, passions, appetites, emotions, feelings, affections, etc.—is completely surrendered. This is what God requires. This is how we fulfill our purpose as humans to know and love Him. And this is the ultimate goal toward which we teach and train our children.

Surrendering your soul to the Lord is an incredible step, positioning you to fulfill God's perfect plan for your life. But you have an enemy, Satan, who has one mission: "to steal, kill, and destroy" (John 10:10 NLT). His war isn't limited to your own soul; he's targeting your children too.

Believers must grasp three vital truths. First, Satan becomes our adversary when we stand with Jesus. In our previous lives of darkness and sin, we weren't a direct threat to him, so he didn't oppose us. However, when we embrace Jesus as "the way, the truth, and the life" (John 14:6), Satan's power over us is broken, and he unleashes war against us.

Second, Satan can't snatch away our salvation, but he can rob us of joy and victory if we remain ignorant of his tactics. We're urged to be vigilant and sober because Satan "walks about like a roaring lion, seeking whom he may devour" (1 Peter 5:8). It's not about salvation but protection. Faith in Jesus saves us, but faith in God's Word protects us. The Bible isn't just a manual for righteous living; it's also our foundation, our weapon, and our guiding light.

Third, we can defend ourselves and our families against Satan's schemes. The key is wholehearted commitment to the Word of God. Ephesians 6 designates the Word as "the sword of the Spirit." It's the only offensive weapon mentioned, and it's all we need. Just as Jesus overcame Satan's temptations by quoting Scripture, a child who cites the Bible wields tremendous spiritual power. The Word of God supersedes any weapon Satan might employ, providing absolute protection.

Our commitment to God's Word doesn't require perfection, which is good, because we will never be perfect on this earth. Satan would love to stop this next generation from growing "in the grace and knowledge of our Lord and Savior Jesus Christ" (2 Peter 3:18), and if he gets the chance to devour your child's soul, he's going to take it. The God of the universe chose *you* to be your child's parent, and you have a God-given duty to fight for that child.

Scripture Reading

The LORD God formed man of the dust of the ground, and breathed into his nostrils the breath of life; and man became a living **soul** (Genesis 2:7 KJV, bold added).

Hear, O Israel: The LORD our God, the LORD *is* one! You shall love the LORD your God with all your heart, with all your soul [*nephesh*], and with all your strength (Deuteronomy 6:4–5).

Jesus replied, "The most important commandment is this: 'Listen, O Israel! The LORD our God is the one and only LORD. And you must love the LORD your

God with all your heart, all your soul [*psuché*], all your mind, and all your strength'" (Mark 12:29–30 NLT).

Discussion Questions

1. How is God's Word our foundation? Our sword? Our light?

2. What does it mean to be committed to God's Word, and what promises does God offer when we make that commitment?

3. What are the different definitions of the Hebrew word *nephesh*? How do they enhance the Scriptures found in this chapter?

Reflection Questions

1. How can you find moments throughout the day to teach the truth of God's Word to your children? What are some examples?

2. How often do you as a family pray with authority against the enemy? Are there areas of tension and strife in your family that need prayer?

3. What Scripture verses or passages do you need now in this season? Ask the Holy Spirit to show them to you and meditate on them.

Connect with the Father

Dear Father, thank You that Your Word protects my soul. Strengthen my faith in You and Your Word more and more so that I can stand against the attacks of the enemy. Teach me so that when doubt comes into my mind, it won't affect me. Protect my family from the enemy. Wherever the devil is trying to cause division, I bind him now in Jesus' name! Amen.

Until Next Time ...

- Read Chapter 4: Dressed to Kill.
- Ask the Lord, "What do You want me to learn from this chapter?"

Dressed to Kill

Recap

- Loving the Lord with all your soul (*nephesh* and *psuché*) means loving Him with everything you have and holding nothing back.

- Satan becomes our adversary when we stand with Jesus.

- Faith in Jesus saves us, but faith in God's Word protects us.

- The God of the universe chose *you* to be your child's parent, and you have a God-given duty to fight for that child.

The Big Idea

Every piece of the armor of God points to Jesus Christ. He is our truth, our righteousness, and our peace. We put our faith in Him, our salvation comes from Him, and His Word defeats the enemy.

Chapter Review

Satan has no legitimate authority or power over your family, but that doesn't stop him from waging a war against you. Like any military conflict, the soul war requires armor. Ephesians 6:10–18 tells us about the six pieces of the armor of God:

Belt of Truth

The belt (*cingulum*) was the central piece of a Roman soldier's armor and served the practical purpose of carrying the scabbard (the sheath) that held the soldier's sword. Without his *cingulum*, a soldier was unprepared and ill-equipped for battle. The same is accurate for believers and truth. Truth not only protects and defends us, but it also defines us. The word Paul uses for truth is *aléthia*. It means 'reality,' 'sincerity,' and 'divine truth revealed to man,'[1] and it's the same word Jesus uses to describe Himself when He says that He is the truth (see John 14:6). Hebrews 13:8 says, "Jesus Christ *is* the same yesterday, today, and forever." Truth is based solely on Him, and because He doesn't change, it doesn't change either.

Breastplate of Righteousness

A Roman soldier's breastplate was made of metal bands that overlapped and were tied together with leather cords. It was light and flexible enough to be worn while running, and it covered the soldier from chest to hips, protecting the vital organs. As believers, we need to understand that our hearts are not naturally good. Righteousness is being right with God, which happens through faith. Paul writes in Romans 3:22, "We are made right with God by placing our faith in Jesus Christ. And this is true for everyone who believes, no matter who we are" (NLT). You can't have righteousness without truth, because you can't be right with God without Jesus. He is "the LORD Our Righteousness" (Jeremiah 23:6 NASB).

Shoes of the Gospel of Peace

Roman soldiers wore *caligae*—sandals made of leather strips attached to a sole that had studs (or spikes) across the bottom. The leather strips were strategically placed not to create blisters, even on long marches, and the studs served the dual purposes of protecting feet from difficult terrain and attacking enemies that had fallen on the ground. The gospel of peace serves as our spiritual battle shoes. The word gospel comes from the Greek *euaggelion*, which means 'good news,' and it always points to Jesus, our Prince of Peace (Isaiah 40:1).

We must prepare our feet with the gospel of peace and march forward.

Shield of Faith

For riding on horseback or fighting hand to hand, a Roman soldier carried a round, 3-foot shield called a *parma*. The other option was the much larger, rectangular *scutum*. It is this second type of shield Paul refers to that could defend not only an individual soldier but also his unit when used together with other such shields. Faith is sincerely believing that Jesus is who He claimed to be and that God will do what He said He would do. Faith is like a muscle, and it grows every time you read the Bible. The basis of our faith is not our emotions, because those will come and go, but rather the unwavering, ever-consistent faithfulness of God.

Helmet of Salvation

A Roman soldier's *galea* served both to protect his head and also to identify him as a particular rank. As believers, we need to understand that our minds are the biggest battlefield of our lives. When Paul writes about salvation in Ephesians 6:17, he is not referring solely to a person's initial moment of surrendering to Christ and being born again. That is a one-time event, after which we must choose to "take" the helmet of salvation and reminds ourselves continually of the incredible hope we have in our

Savior. By taking the helmet of salvation, we declare our allegiance to Jesus and our faith that His perfect work on the cross will result in eternal life.

Sword of the Spirit

The Greek word Paul uses is *machaira*, or "a short sword or dagger"[2] that has an extremely sharp blade designed to be used in hand-to-hand combat. The Word of God is our *machaira* against the enemy. It lights our path (Psalm 119:105), defeats temptation (Matthew 4:1–11), removes condemnation (Romans 8:1), and guarantees salvation (John 3:16; Hebrews 7:25). The Word of God absolutely decimates the enemy, which is why Satan tries everything he can to prevent believers from understanding its power.

Because Satan is the "father of lies," he has no trouble spotting another liar (John 8:44 NIV). The only way to make him think you're wearing the armor of God is for you to actually wear the armor of God. And the only way to wear the armor of God is to have a relationship with Jesus Christ.

Scripture Reading

Finally, be strong in the Lord and in the strength of His might. Put on the full armor of God, so that you will be able to stand firm against the schemes of the devil. For our struggle is not against flesh and blood, but against the rulers, against the powers, against the world forces of this darkness, against the spiritual *forces* of wickedness in the heavenly *places*. Therefore, take up the full armor of God, so that you will be able to resist on the evil day, and having done everything, to stand firm. Stand firm therefore, having belted your waist with truth, and having put on the breastplate of righteousness, and having strapped on your feet the preparation of the gospel of peace; in addition to all, taking up the shield of faith with which you will be able to extinguish all the flaming arrows of the evil *one*. And take the helmet of salvation and the sword of the Spirit, which is the word of God (Ephesians 6:10–18 NASB).

We are made right with God by placing our faith in Jesus Christ. And this is true for everyone who believes, no matter who we are (Romans 3:22 NLT).

But since we belong to the day, let us be sober, putting on faith and love as a breastplate, and **the hope of salvation as a helmet**. For God did not appoint us to suffer wrath but to receive salvation through our Lord Jesus Christ. He died for us so that, whether we are awake or asleep, we may live together with him (1 Thessalonians 5:8–10 NIV, bold added).

Discussion Questions

1. Why is truth described as a belt? How is the breastplate of righteousness connected to the belt of truth?

2. What does it mean to strap your feet with the "preparation of the gospel of peace"? How does the good news of God's Word ground us?

3. What is the importance of the helmet of salvation? Why is the mind the biggest battlefield of our lives?

Reflection Questions

1. Where do you still struggle with fully trusting in God's Word? How can you anchor yourself in His truth?

2. Where is your hope placed? Do you see the hope of salvation as a dream that may or may not turn out? Or is your hope grounded in confident expectation of Christ's faithfulness?

3. Is there an area where your thoughts tend to be unguarded and open to attack? How can you better protect your mind?

Connect with the Father

Dear Father, thank You for providing me with armor so that I can be protected in spiritual warfare. Gird me with truth. Help me believe that I am righteous in Your sight. Keep me grounded in Your good news. Shield me with Your Word. Constantly remind me of my salvation. Teach me to wield Your Word like a sword. And help me to teach my children to do the same. In Jesus' name, Amen.

Until Next Time ...

- Read Chapter 5: Weapons Check.
- Ask the Lord, "What do You want me to learn from this chapter?"

Chapter 5 Guide

Weapons Check

Recap

- The soul war requires the armor of God:

    o Belt of Truth
    o Breastplate of Righteousness
    o Shoes of the Gospel of Peace
    o Shield of Faith
    o Helmet of Salvation
    o Sword of the Spirit

- The only way to make Satan think you're wearing the armor of God is for you to actually wear the armor of God.

The Big Idea

Fighting for the soul of your child isn't about being a good parent raising a good kid. It's about being a *godly* parent raising a *godly* kid. You can't be godly without God.

Chapter Review

Are you ready to fight for your children? If you know Jesus as your Lord and Savior, the answer is yes. If not, you face a critical decision that impacts your parenting and life.

Spiritual death and the natural tendency to rebel against God are inherent in every person. Jesus, the Son of God, came to earth, lived a sinless life, and died the most painful death imaginable on the cross in order to pay for the sins of all mankind. Then, three days later, He rose again, having defeated the power of sin and death once and for all.

Being "born again" (also called being "saved") is a free gift you receive instantly when you open your heart to Jesus and accept Him as your Lord and Savior. He will forgive all your sins, allowing you to have the relationship with God you were created to enjoy. He will give you the gift of eternal life in heaven, and He will take you with Him when He comes back to gather His people.

There are two crucial issues to understand in becoming a true believer in Christ. First, without acknowledging the lordship of Christ, we are simply buying "fire insurance" to save us from hell and make us feel better. A profession of faith that doesn't acknowledge Christ as Lord doesn't change the fundamental problem between God and us—rebellion (see Matthew 7:22–23). Also, believing that God raised Jesus from the dead is essential because it signifies that only Jesus, and no other so-called savior, guru, or religious leader, satisfied the requirements of God to save us from our sins. The resurrection was God's public and eternal validation that Jesus was who He said He was and that His sacrifice for our sins was accepted.

Salvation occurs as we believe and confess in accordance with God's will. That is all we have to do. Jesus did the hard part for us that we never could have done. Now, by believing and confessing, we can freely receive salvation from God. There is nothing we can do to deserve it. We can only accept it or reject it.

Are you ready to invite Jesus to be your Lord and Savior? If so, pray this prayer:

Father God, I confess that I have sinned against You, and I repent. I believe that You sent Your Son, Jesus, to pay the price for my sins and to restore my relationship with You. Jesus, I accept You as my Lord and Savior. I submit my life to You, and from this day forward I will live to serve You. I believe You have come into my heart and have forgiven me of my sins. I believe I am now saved by Your grace. I have the gift of eternal life, and I am now ready for Your return. Jesus, I pray You will fill me with Your Holy Spirit and

give me the power to change, know You, and live my
life for You. Amen!

If you sincerely prayed that prayer, then congratulations! You can be sure that God heard you, and Jesus is now the Lord and Savior of your life. You are eternally changed, and your salvation is secure in Christ. Your name has been written in the book of life in heaven (see Philippians 4:3; Revelation 21:27). Believing in Jesus involves confessing Him as Lord, recognizing Him as the only way to salvation, experiencing transformation, hearing God's voice, relying on grace, embracing His Word, and demonstrating love for fellow believers. These seven signs mark a genuine faith in Christ according to biblical passages.

Surrendering own your life to God is the essential first step to fighting for your child's soul. There are billions of non-Christian parents all over the world who love their kids and do their very best to protect and provide for them and raise up them to be decent people. However, salvation is critical for godly parenting because your children won't be more spiritual than you are. You might be able to force your child to do what you say while they are young and dependent on you for their every need, but as soon as they realize that you don't "do" it yourself, the countdown to rebellion is on. Your life will always speak louder than your lips.

Scripture Reading

"If you abide in My word, you are My disciples indeed. And you shall know the truth, and the truth shall make you free" (John 8:31–32).

If you declare with your mouth, "Jesus is Lord," and believe in your heart that God raised him from the dead, you will be saved. For it is with your heart that you believe and are justified, and it is with your mouth that you profess your faith and are saved (Romans 10:9–10 NIV).

Therefore, if anyone *is* in Christ, *he is* a new creation; old things have passed away; behold, all things have become new (2 Corinthians 5:17).

A new commandment I give to you, that you love one another; as I have loved you, that you also love one another. By this all will know that you are My disciples, if you have love for one another (John 13:34–35).

Discussion Questions

1. How do you think a person's life and priorities change once they sincerely accept Jesus as their Lord and Savior? What kinds of changes does Scripture describe?

2. How can abiding in God's Word help us grow as disciples of Jesus?

3. Why is loving others an essential mark of following Jesus? What makes this kind of love distinct?

4. In what ways can parents reflect Christ and point their children to Him through their words and actions?

Reflection Questions

1. Do you have full assurance that you are a child of God and possess eternal life? If not, what is causing you to doubt your salvation?

2. In what ways have you experienced the loving kindness and mercy of God this week? How can you reflect that grace to others?

3. Do you recognize God's voice and seek to follow His leading daily? What helps you better attune your ear to His voice?

4. In what ways do you still try to earn salvation or God's favor through good works? How can you rely more fully on His grace?

Connect with the Father

Dear Father, thank You for sending Your Son, Jesus, to bring forgiveness and mercy. Take control of my life and transform me into the person You want me to be.

Help me to daily surrender to Your leading. Open my ears to Your voice. Empower me with Your Spirit and establish Your Word within me so that I may stand firm against the lies of the enemy. Make me a parent after Your own heart, with the wisdom to raise my children to know and love You. I commit their lives and souls to You. In Jesus' name, Amen.

Until Next Time …

- Read Chapter 6: Missile Launch
- Ask the Lord, "What do You want me to learn from this chapter?"

Chapter 6 Guide

Missile Launch

Recap

- How do you know you're saved?

    o Confessing with your mouth that Jesus is Lord.
    o Believing that Jesus is the only way to salvation.
    o Experiencing transformation.
    o Hearing God's voice.
    o Relying on God's grace.
    o Relying on the Word of God.
    o Loving fellow believers.

- By surrendering your life to Jesus, you take another step in securing your child's soul.

The Big Idea

Unforgiveness is a torpedo that launches from your past, destroys your present, and erases your future. You need to disarm it before it can do any further damage to you and your child.

Chapter Review

The enemy uses plenty of weapons against godly parents, but the most subtle torpedo is unforgiveness. To say so is not a case of being "holier-than-thou." God's Word makes this clear.

How many times must we forgive before we're off the hook? Jesus told Peter, "Up to seventy times seven." But Jesus was not being literal. Instead, His point was that forgiveness is unlimited, especially when we understand how God has forgiven us.

In Matthew 18:21–35, Jesus tells the story of a servant (let's name him George) who owed his master a massive amount of money—10,000 talents, which is equal to $3 billion. George was unable to pay off this debt and begged his master for mercy, knowing that he, his wife, and his children would otherwise be sold into slavery. Miraculously, the master forgave his debt. But immediately after, George found a fellow servant (we'll call him Sam) and demanded that Sam pay him the 100 denarii—equal to about $10,000— at once. Sam was unable to pay George, so George throws him into prison until the debt is repaid.

When the master found out what George did to Sam, he revoked the forgiveness of George's debt and turned George over to the torturers. *Torture* is a pretty strong word, but unforgiveness truly is a torturous lifestyle. According to a Johns Hopkins Medicine article, chronic anger can affect heart rate, blood pressure, and immune response, leading to an increased risk of depression, heart disease, and diabetes, among other conditions.[1] In addition, anger left unchecked leaves an opening to the enemy who wants to bring division into your relationships and demonic torment into your life.

By giving place to unforgiveness, we also give place to destructive behaviors: revenge, hatred, verbal abuse, divorce, rejection and avoidance for punishment's sake, withholding good, transferring affection, prejudice, bigotry, racism, sexism, bitterness, wishing evil on someone, or praying against someone. Therefore, though unforgiveness may seem justified, it is not. Unforgiveness is the devil's territory and hurts your relationship with the Lord. And if we do not forgive others, God says He will not forgive our sins (see Matthew 6:15). All of us have done bad things repeatedly and are in need of forgiveness that we cannot earn and do not deserve. That is why Jesus died on the cross. Understanding that we are forgiven helps us to forgive others.

Forgiving those who really hurt you is a threefold process. First, repent to God for harboring long-term anger or bitterness toward someone. Second, release the offender from your judgment, trusting God to deal with that individual instead. Finally, bless the offender until your feelings toward them change. This last step breaks the cycle of hate from your life, because no one can wish good upon someone they hate. It may take some time for change to take place within you, but be encouraged. If you will obey God in blessing and praying for those who have offended you or those you love, He will be faithful to heal your emotions so you can go forward with a renewed heart.

Scripture Reading

"Love your enemies, do good to those who hate you, bless those who curse you, and pray for those who spitefully use you" (Luke 6:27–28).

"Be angry, and do not sin"; do not let the sun go down on your wrath, nor give place to the devil (Ephesians 4:26–27).

And forgive us our debts, as we forgive our debtors (Matthew 6:12).

Discussion Questions

1. How might unforgiveness "give place to the devil"? What makes it so spiritually dangerous?

2. Why do you think we sometimes enjoy holding onto bitterness and anger? What makes it so tempting?

3. How can a parent's example of forgiveness have a lasting impact on their children? Why is this important?

Reflection Questions

1. Is there anyone from your past you need to forgive? What feelings arise as you reflect on the hurt they caused?

2. Do you trust God to deal justly with those who have hurt you? Or do you feel like you need to punish them yourself? What does your response reveal?

3. Do you truly believe that Jesus has completely forgiven you of all your sins? According to Scripture, how great is His forgiveness and love toward you?

Connect with the Father

Dear Father, thank You for Your unconditional love and forgiveness. Forgive me for holding onto bitterness and anger against those who have hurt me. Today, I choose to forgive them. I release them into Your righteous judgment. I pray that You bless them in every area of their lives and cause them to prosper. As I come to understand how much You love me, let it affect my attitude and actions so that my children see You in and through me. In Jesus' name, Amen.

Until Next Time …

- Read Chapter 7: Free to Fight
- Ask the Lord, "What do You want me to learn from this chapter?"

Chapter 7 Guide

Free to Fight

Recap

- Unforgiveness is a silent killer and hurts your relationship with the Lord.

- Jesus forgives us unconditionally.

- Disarm the torpedo of unforgiveness by:

  o Repenting of your bitterness.
  o Releasing the offender from your judgment.
  o Blessing the offender until you mean it.

The Big Idea

Both generational sins and inner vows made in response to pain keep us in bondage. These must be broken from our lives so that we and our children can be free from the enemy's control.

Chapter Review

Just as your child won't be more spiritual than you, your child also won't be more free than you. If you are in bondage to iniquities and inner vows, your ability to fight for your child will be hindered.

"Iniquities" are sins that have been passed down from generation to generation. They are the negative behaviors that children see every day from their parents until they are ingrained in them. Just as Adam and Eve's sin has affected every generation of people on this planet, the sinful behaviors of our parents will negatively influence our lives. Abusive or dominant behaviors are frequently learned from parents and generational family systems. Without intervention, iniquities will always pass on to the next generation.

Praise the Lord that iniquities can be broken! The first step is to recognize the iniquities of your parents, those areas where they failed to represent God's character. Once those are identified, forgive your parents, realizing that the baggage they passed down to you was probably also passed down to them. Then submit this area of your life to Jesus. Pray, "Lord, I repent of this tendency, and I submit it to You." He is faithful to redeem your life. Declare, "In the name of Jesus, I break this iniquity over my life." Believe it is done. If you continue to struggle in this area, talk about it to someone you trust. In Christ, you will see your freedom.

"Inner vows" are promises we make to ourselves, often in response to pain, difficulty, or frustration. We may say to ourselves, "No one will ever hurt me again," or "I will do better with my children" in order to comfort ourselves concerning the future. By doing so, we are not trying to do wrong. We are trying to prevent evil from happening again. But inner vows are unscriptural because in any area we swear to ourselves, Jesus isn't the Lord of that area—we are (see Matthew 5:33–37).

The significant commitments of our lives are meant to be focused on God as acts of worship and obedience to Him. But inner vows are self-focused, self-serving promises that often resist and oppose the will of God in our lives. Under the influence of an inner vow, you become unteachable, unapproachable, and irrational. Anything that seems to threaten your vow will cause you to overreact or overcorrect out of fear. Worse, it takes the place of God in your life. When we are driven by inner vows, we replace our commitment to Christ with them and make them our highest priority.

Inner vows may be hard to recognize because there is pain attached to them, but the Holy Spirit can reveal them to you and free you from their influence. Once you become aware of them, renounce them as sin and submit this area of your life to the Lord. Forgive everybody associated with the vow—whoever it was who inspired you to make the vow in the first place. Finally, bind and cast out every demon spirit that took control over your life through each vow you made. It may take some time to see complete freedom. This is warfare! But Jesus promises you freedom. And when you are free, you will be able to fight for the soul of your child.

Scripture Reading

"The Lord, the Lord God, merciful and gracious, longsuffering, and abounding in goodness and truth, keeping mercy for thousands, forgiving iniquity and transgression and sin, by no means clearing *the guilty*, visiting the iniquity of the fathers upon the children and the children's children to the third and fourth generation" (Exodus 34:6–7).

Let your "Yes" be "Yes," and your "No," "No." For whatever is more than these is from the evil one (Matthew 5:37).

Confess *your* trespasses to one another, and pray for one another, that you may be healed. The effective, fervent prayer of a righteous man avails much (James 5:16).

Discussion Questions

1. What happens if iniquities go unaddressed from generation to generation? How can we break the cycle?

2. Why are inner vows "from the evil one"? How can they affect our children?

3. How could walking in freedom from iniquities and inner vows empower your parenting? What impact could this have?

Reflection Questions

1. What sins or bondages have you observed in your family history that you need to have broken over your life?

2. Is there any bitterness in your heart toward your parents or ancestors that is hindering your freedom?

3. Are there any inner vows governing your choices or habits that you need to renounce and submit to God?

4. How could walking in freedom strengthen your life, marriage, and family?

Connect with the Father

Dear Father, thank You for complete freedom by the blood of Jesus. I submit to You every iniquity and inner vow that have governed my life. I no longer want them to have power over me. Jesus, You are Lord. Help me to release control over my life to You. Help me to walk in freedom so that I may raise my children for Your glory. In Jesus' name, Amen.

Until Next Time ...

- Read Chapter 8: Chain of Command
- Ask the Lord, "What do You want me to learn from this chapter?"

Chapter 8 Guide

Chain of Command

Recap

- Iniquities are sins and bondages passed down from generation to generation. Break free by:

  o Recognizing the iniquities of your parents.
  o Forgiving your parents.
  o Repenting and submitting that area of your life to Jesus Christ.
  o Breaking its hold over your life.

- Inner vows are promises we make to ourselves in times of pain, difficulty, or frustration. Break free by:

  o Renouncing the inner vow.
  o Submitting that area of your life to the Lord.
  o Forgiving everyone associated with the vow.
  o Binding the evil spirit associated with it.

The Big Idea

God has established a chain of command in His ranks, and it must be followed to the letter. This law of priority is in place to protect your relationship with God and your family.

Chapter Review

Being in an army requires fitting within the chain of command. Since Christians are the army of God, God's kingdom has its own chain of command. And it is not a suggestion. It is a *law* of priority. When you obey God's law of priority, you place yourself directly under the protection of His Word. Doing things your own way, on the other hand, means you lose your protection and authority over the enemy.

The kingdom's chain of command is as follows: God, spouse, children. This means while fighting for your child, you must also fight for your spouse and for your relationship with God.

It is one thing to claim to love God. It is another matter entirely to have a true relationship with Him. Though loving people is important, God created us to love and serve Him first. When we give time that rightfully belongs to Him to someone or something else, we provoke Him to legitimate jealousy. When we give Him the first (and best) of our time and money (tithe), we show that we love Him. Loving God isn't about perfection—it's about sacrifice.

What we sacrifice never belonged to us in the first place. Everything belongs to God. And nothing we give up will ever equal the sacrifice Jesus made on the cross for us. Only through Him can we have a relationship with our heavenly Father. When we wake up in the morning and give the first of the day to Him, He goes forward in time and prepares the way for the rest of the day.

God designed marriage as the most important human relationship in our lives, second only to our relationship with Him. This means your spouse takes precedence over all other relationships because you and your spouse are *one*. Countless relationships have ended in divorce because something else was prioritized over their marriage. This is because when one spouse's time, energy, and resources are being given to someone or something else, the other spouse has been violated, and they will feel legitimate jealousy. Even making your children more important than your spouse is a violation, and your spouse may turn their attention to their career or other interests outside the home as a result. Then no one is prioritizing the marriage, which is a violation of God's design for marriage.

After your relationship with God and your spouse, your children are the most important thing in your life. They come before work, church, hobbies, extended family members, friends, etc. Vocational ministry is sometimes confused with having a relationship with God. But while your relationship with

God comes first, your vocation (even ministry) comes *after* your spouse and children.

Children learn everywhere they go, and you are not the only one influencing them. If your child begins to act out, you may need to put some boundaries around their friendships. No one has the *right* to play with our children. That is a special privilege. If the person—a cousin, a neighbor, or a child of a church member—does not have good character, they should have limited contact with your child. This applies to the parents as well.

The greatest threats to your relationship with God, your spouse, and your children aren't bad things—they're good things out of priority.

Scripture Reading

Yet indeed I also count all things loss for the excellence of the knowledge of Christ Jesus my Lord, for whom I have suffered the loss of all things, and count them as rubbish, that I may gain Christ (Philippians 3:8).

Therefore a man shall leave his father and mother and be joined to his wife, and they shall become one flesh (Genesis 2:24).

But the Advocate, the Holy Spirit, whom the Father will send in my name, will teach you all things and will remind you of everything I have said to you (John 14:26 NIV).

Behold, children *are* a heritage from the LORD,
The fruit of the womb *is* a reward (Psalm 127:3).

Discussion Questions

1. Why does the Bible establish a chain of command? How does it protect relationships?

2. What makes God jealous? How should we understand godly jealousy?

3. How can parents balance being involved with their children while still prioritizing their marriage?

4. How should parents be involved in their children's lives on a regular basis?

Reflection Questions

1. Are there any "little gods" in your life that are competing with your devotion to God? What can you do to reprioritize?

2. Do you date your spouse and devote focused time to know their heart? If not, what can you do differently this week to reconnect?

3. How can you create more quality bonding time with your kids each week? What fun activities can you plan?

Connect with the Father

Dear Father, I place You first before everything else in my life. If there is anything that I have made more important than You, I repent of it. You are the most important. Help me to strengthen my relationship with You. Thank You for my spouse. Help me to love him/ her better than ever. Thank You also for my children; they are a true gift from You. Give me wisdom to guard them well. And help me remember that they are in Your hands. In Jesus' name, Amen.

Until Next Time …

- Read Chapter 9: A Biblical Worldview
- Ask the Lord, "What do You want me to learn from this chapter?"

Section 2

BOOT CAMP

Chapter 9 Guide

A Biblical Worldview

Recap

- There is a chain of command in the kingdom of God:

    o God
    o Spouse
    o Children

- Giving God the first of your time and money shows your love for Him.

- Your marriage should always be prioritized over your children.

- Get to know your children well and learn who they hang out with so that you can guard them well.

The Big Idea

God's Word is truth. We do not have the authority to pick and choose the parts we like best and
throwing away the rest. As parents, we must raise
our children with Scripture as our guide and Jesus
as our Lord.

Chapter Review

In the parable of the Ten Virgins, Jesus says that
half the Church will fall away in the end times
(see Matthew 25:1–13). In this parable, the bridegroom represents Jesus, and the virgins represent
the Church. With this very thing happening before
our eyes, it is important to teach our children from
Scripture. This does not mean pressuring them
into salvation. As much as we love our children, we
have to realize that we are not the fourth member
of the Trinity. It is up to the Holy Spirit to soften
their hearts and open their eyes to their need for
salvation.

Once your children are saved, Satan will do
everything he can to steal the joy and victory that
come from truly knowing and loving God. After
all, there is a difference between *knowing about*
someone and really knowing them. That is the sig-
nificance of having a biblical worldview. Everyone
has a worldview. According to Dr. George Barna,
Director of Research and cofounder of the Cultural

Research Center (CRC) at Arizona Christian University (ACU), a worldview determines how we operate in daily life. If that's the case, then a biblical worldview determines our daily life according to the Bible. Based on statistics from the CRC, 68 percent of American adults claim to be Christians, but only 6 percent have a biblical worldview, and only 1 percent of adults under 30 years old have a biblical worldview.[1] American society is becoming increasingly hostile toward biblical principles. And many who think they are Christians are only Christian by name. The ancient Greeks used the word *nomizo* to refer to beliefs people held purely out of custom, such as faith inherited from family members. That describes many in our society who call themselves Christians. The sad reality is that many people who attend church may not actually know Jesus.

According to Dr. Barna, "a parent's primary responsibility is to prepare a child for the life God intends for that child. A crucial element in that nurturing is helping the child develop a biblical worldview—the filter that causes a person to make their choices in harmony with biblical teachings and principles.... The typical American parent is either fully unaware that there is a worldview development process, or they are aware that their child is developing a worldview, but they do not take responsibility for a role in the process.... Or they are aware the child's worldview is being developed, but choose or allow outsiders to accomplish that duty on the parent's behalf."[2] If we as parents do not intentionally speak into our children's lives, we should not be surprised when we see them struggling in school, with relationships, or with their faith. The fault lies with us.

However, it is not a matter of striving for perfect church attendance. We attend church and memorize Scripture because those things help us to know and love God, who made us in His image. With this mindset, we help our children do the same. To teach biblical principles as absolutes is not "imposing" our views on our children. Society will tell you that it is, and that you are oppressing your children. But it is not. It is fighting for their souls. Of course, there have been people who have been legitimately hurt by leaders in the Church, and that is a terrible thing. But just because our society does not like what God's Word teaches does not make it "toxic" or "old-fashioned." Sin is truly "toxic." Society does not determine what is good or moral—God does. Without Him, we are doomed to eternal separation from our Creator. But Jesus is the way, the truth, and the life (see John 14:6). Only He can save us. We cannot save ourselves. Neither can we handpick Scriptures that make us feel good and reject those we don't like. The whole of Scripture should be our standard. This doesn't mean you will be a perfect parent. It means that you committed to living your life and raising your children with the

Word of God as your standard and Jesus Christ as your Lord and Savior.

Scripture Reading

Enter by the narrow gate; for wide *is* the gate and broad *is* the way that leads to destruction, and there are many who go in by it (Matthew 7:13).

You shall teach them diligently to your children, and shall talk of them when you sit in your house, when you walk by the way, when you lie down, and when you rise up (Deuteronomy 6:7).

For the message of the cross is foolishness to those who are perishing, but to us who are being saved it is the power of God (1 Corinthians 1:18).

Discussion Questions

1. What's the difference between knowing *about* God and truly knowing *Him*? How can we move from one to the other?

2. How can parents teach biblical principles through their own example? What are some practical ways to do this?

3. Why is it dangerous to determine right and wrong by society's standards? How does a biblical worldview establish morality?

Reflection Questions

1. In what ways have you relied on culture to instill values in your kids? How can you take more responsibility?

2. What biblical teachings do you find difficult or uncomfortable? What could you learn from them?

3. Are there times when you have watered down or compromised biblical truths to avoid criticism from others?

Connect with the Father

Dear Father, thank You for Your Word. Thank You that it is a lamp to my feet and a light to my path. Help me to live out Your Word for my children so that they may know You. Give me discernment to teach them properly and effectively. And give me boldness for You in this troubled world. In Jesus' name, Amen.

Until Next Time …

- Read Chapter 10: Who Am I?

- Ask the Lord, "What do You want me to learn from this chapter?"

Who Am I?

Recap

- The Greek word *nomizo* refers to beliefs people held purely out of custom, such as faith inherited from family members.

- Many "Christians" in our society are only Christian by name.

- Parents are responsible for nurturing their children spiritually, no matter what the world might say about our faith.

The Big Idea

Knowing who you are in Christ gives you an unshakable identity. You become a more confident person, and you are better equipped as a parent to protect and defend your children.

Chapter Review

You have a name, an age, a certain look, and a certain way of talking. But your identity goes deeper than all of that. It goes deeper than even your job, your education, your relationships, or your political associations. But if that's true, then who are you?

If you base your identity on your abilities, your social status, or your relationships—any factor of your life that can change in a moment—then the enemy has an open door into your life to cause disappointment, confusion, and heartache. Your identity will only be secure if it is based on your relationship with God. Who does He say you are? Because God never changes, what He says never changes either.

Your identity in Christ—in other words, your *union* in Christ—is the most stable aspect of your life. If you want to know who you are, then you need to know who God is and why He sent His Son, Jesus. So who is God?

The Bible describes God in five ways, which are repeated over and over from Genesis to Revelation. He is a Father, a Bridegroom, a Messenger of the Good News, a Person whom we can know, and a King.

God created Adam and Eve to have relationship with Him and to do His will. But they lost that relationship after they sinned. Their identity was distorted. Jesus Christ restores our relationship with God and our identity as individuals and as the Church. And He will perfect that identity when He comes again.

What identity was restored to us? Our identity as the *sons* of God. The use of the word "sons" is important, not because it excludes women from being daughters of God but because calling the women "sons" means that they too receive the inheritance of the kingdom of God. In the ancient world, daughters didn't receive the inheritance. Only sons did. By calling both men and women "sons of God," the Bible is setting them on equal ground. Jesus paid the price for all of us to be set free from our sins. We can cry out, "Abba! Father!"

Let that sink in. You are no longer considered a stranger to God. You are a new creation in Christ Jesus (see 2 Corinthians 5:17)! The Creator of the universe is your Dad, and you are His son! And He delights in you and provides for all of your needs (see Zephaniah 3:17 and Philippians 4:19).

The Bible tells us that we were created in the image of God. Evolution, on the other hand, says that we were created in the image of the last organism from which we evolved, sin is a social construct from which we need no redemption, and death is the absolute end of existence. In other words, evolutionary theory strips us of our God-given identity. It puts us on the same level as animals. Satan would love to strip you of your identity in Christ. But God personally formed us and knew us even before we were born (see Psalm 139:13–18). Animals are part of God's creation, but they are not our equals. You are divinely made, beloved by God, and special. You have great value because you are a son of the living God!

Scripture Reading

"If you abide in My word, you are My disciples indeed. And you shall know the truth, and the truth shall make you free" (John 8:31–32).

Behold, what manner of love the Father hath bestowed upon us, that we should be called the sons of God (1 John 3:1 KJV).

And because you are sons, God has sent forth the Spirit of His Son into your hearts, crying out "Abba, Father!" Therefore you are no longer a slave but a son, and if a son, then an heir of God through Christ (Galatians 4:6–7).

For as many as are led by the Spirit of God, these are sons of God. For you did not receive the spirit of bondage again to fear, but you received the Spirit of adoption by whom we cry out, "Abba, Father" (Romans 8:14–15).

Discussion Questions

1. Why is it important for us to understand who God is in order to understand our identity in Christ?

2. What is the importance of believers being called "sons" instead of "children" of God?

3. How does knowing your identity in Christ help you live more confidently?

4. Why is the theory of evolution a problem when it comes to our identity?

Reflection Questions

1. Do I allow my identity to be shaped by cultural values or my circumstances?

2. Do I start my day remembering who I am in Christ? Would this affect how I face challenges?

3. How can I help others discover their God-given identity?

Connect with the Father

Dear Father, help me let go of everything I know or think I know about myself. Give me a fresh revelation of who I am in Christ and who You made me to be.

Thank You for making me Your son with an amazing inheritance. Thank You that I can live confident of Your love for me. You created me in Your image, and that is enough for me. In Jesus' name, Amen.

Until Next Time …

- Read Chapter 11: United We Stand

- Ask the Lord, "What do You want me to learn from this chapter?"

United We Stand

Recap

- We are made in the image of God.

- Our identity in Christ defines who we are.

- As sons of God, we receive the inheritance of the kingdom through Christ Jesus.

The Big Idea

Your marriage is important enough to prioritize now. Parenting well requires a unified front so that you can model a healthy marriage for your kids.

Chapter Review

Why wait for the kids to be out of the house to work on your marriage? After all that time, you would have years of resentment, frustration, and disappointment to deal with. Better to do the work now for the sake of your marriage *and* for your kids' sake.

We realize that some people reading this are single parents. If that's you, then please know that we love you so much, and we never want you to feel left out or ostracized. If you ever desire to be married in the future, now is the time to prepare.

For a successful marriage, you need to close ranks! That means to band together in a unified stand, especially against challenges. This is you and your spouse standing shoulder to shoulder or, even better, face to face, in order to protect your family.

Sometimes, the best dividers are children, the master manipulators. Especially when dealing with them, you must be united as a two-headed monster. You and your spouse may not always agree on everything, but at all costs, it is best never to disagree in front of the kids. In order to be a successful two-headed monster, you and your spouse need to figure out what you believe. What are your core values? And what areas can be compromised? Just remember not to compromise in front of the children. What they should see is a united front—each parent gives them the same amount of affection and concern and the same sort of discipline.

By having parenting conversations behind closed doors and being respectful to each other in the open, what your kids see is your honor and respect for one another. Whether you speak kindly or sarcastically to each other, your children will notice. And they will do the same thing.

Children want your undivided attention 24/7 with unrestricted access. In order to maintain a healthy marriage, your children must be taught to respect your marriage. This means creating boundaries. You will always love your children, but raising them is a temporary assignment. Your marriage will last longer, so it needs to take priority (but remember that God takes first priority). Take time to be alone together, to talk, and to be sexually intimate. Just make sure your kid doesn't know how to pick the lock on your bedroom door!

A successful marriage is not about what you can make happen once. Anyone can manage to do almost anything once, but it's not guaranteed to happen again. If your marriage is sinking, the goal is to get it back on track and keep it there. Develop new disciplines and traditions that make your spouse the priority again. You're not a bad parent if you take a few days away from your kids every so often to spend time together. In fact, your kids will probably enjoy it as much as you do, and they will definitely benefit from it.

Here are some good disciplines and traditions to build into your marriage to keep you close and ensure that both of your needs are met in a prioritized and energetic manner:

- A weekly date night
- Praying together and going to church
- Taking walks together
- Taking short, overnight, or weekend trips
- Talking face-to-face without distractions every day
- Planning times to have sex when you are both rested
- Not going to bed angry (talking things out and forgiving each other)
- Reading a marriage book together
- Going to a marriage conference
- Watching a romantic comedy together
- Finding something you both enjoy doing and doing it regularly

Children are smart and observant. If there is tension in your relationship, they will notice it and internalize it. If you and your spouse are stuck in a long-term struggle with seemingly no way out, go outside your marriage for counseling and input. This does *not* include posting about your marriage on social media or gossiping about your spouse's problems with all your friends. Instead, seek out a biblically sound, trustworthy authority figure who can help you navigate the issue. Remember, you're human. There are going to be issues that you can't solve on your own. Getting help is not a sign of weakness; it's a sign of wisdom. In all things, remain teachable.

Parenting takes faith, especially in today's world. You're not a bad parent if your child tests boundaries. Sometimes the results of your parenting don't show themselves until your child is an adult. In the meantime, until they move out, it is important to model a solid, healthy marriage to them as best you can and with God's help.

Scripture Reading

If a house is divided against itself, that house cannot stand (Mark 3:25).

Be very careful, then, how you live—not as unwise but as wise, making the most of every opportunity, because the days are evil (Ephesians 5:15–16 NIV).

And be kind to one another, tenderhearted, forgiving one another, even as God in Christ forgave you (Ephesians 4:32).

Discussion Questions

1. Why is it important for parents to "close ranks" and be unified? What are some ways they can do this effectively?

2. How do children try to divide their parents? What strategies can parents use to counteract this?

3. How can married couples make their relationship a priority while raising kids? What disciplines or traditions could help?

Reflection Questions

1. Do your children have healthy boundaries and respect for your marriage? If not, what is one boundary you need to address?

2. In what ways are you still putting unrealistic expectations on yourself as a parent? How can you release that pressure?

3. How has parenting stretched your faith? What has God taught you through your children lately?

Connect with the Father

Dear Father, give me the strength and humility to be fully united with my spouse, especially for the sake of our children. Help us to model Your love to them. We place You at the center of our marriage. Bless our marriage so that we can be good examples for our children. And help us to become better at setting boundaries for the sake of our relationship. In Jesus' name, Amen.

Until Next Time …

- Read Chapter 12: Joining Ranks
- Ask the Lord, "What do You want me to learn from this chapter?"

Chapter 12 Guide

Joining Ranks

Recap

- The time to work on your marriage is now, while the kids are still in the house.

- Stand as a united front for your children to see.

- Prioritize your relationship with your spouse.

- Parenting takes faith.

The Big Idea

Blended families face unique challenges. But they can be overcome by keeping marriage as the priority.

Chapter Review

The traditional family is nuclear, with the marriage as the nucleus around which the rest of the family is built. In this sort of family, it's much easier to prioritize marriage.

However, the number of blended families in the US is on the rise, In these relationships, it's tempting to make the children the nucleus. But this will only lead to disaster. Divorce rates are higher in second, third, and subsequent marriages. So regardless of what came first, marriage must be the center of the family because that is how God designed it.

The common mindset in blended families is, "My children are permanent, but my new spouse may not be." That is an immediate sign of trouble. And often, this idea is created by the fear that your children will not be happy with your new marriage. If you don't trust your new spouse to raise your children, then you probably shouldn't marry them in the first place. If you do trust them, then how well you commit to your marriage will determine the security and happiness of your children.

Like the law of priority, there is another law that must be obeyed for a marriage to be successful—the *law of partnership*. God designed marriage to be a complete joining and sharing of two lives. These two lives meld and become one. In other words, when you marry someone, they become co-owners of everything in your life. Yes, this includes the children. The new spouse should never replace the other biological parent. Not at all. But the new spouse *should* be an equal parent, with the right to speak into the children's lives. The greatest love on earth—*agape*—is a decision, not an emotion. It is love by choice. Just as God chooses to love us, your spouse can choose to love your children like you do, and you can choose to love their children like they do.

As far as discipline is concerned, it is typically better for the biological parent to discipline their children, especially when the marriage is new. Even in this area, though, the new spouse must be allowed to work with you as a team. A healthy blended family calls the children "*ours.*"

Blended families tend to experience some unique issues:

- **Modesty** – Sexual attraction is more likely between non-biological family members than between biological siblings. Without encouraging mistrust, it is wise to have higher standards of modesty. Use common sense. No one should be walking around naked or in their underwear, especially around the opposite sex.

- **Accountability** – If you or your spouse have children from a previous marriage that need to be supported, the non-biological spouse should agree to take on the debts, assets, and liabilities of the related spouse. Joining in marriage means agreeing to support your spouse's children with a good attitude.

- **Visitation** – If an ex-spouse is spoiling the children or turning them against you, do not use the children as your messengers. Communicate directly with your ex-spouse. When your children leave your home, pray over them that their hearts and minds be protected from corruption. Believe that God will protect them. And when you have time with your children, don't take a moment for granted. Be fun and be righteous. Love them and don't lower your standards. Take them to church. Never underestimate the power of God to impact their hearts. And when those children mature, they'll bless you for your righteousness.

Our children are our legacy, which the devil wants to destroy. To protect this legacy—a Kingdom legacy!—we fight to break generational curses. We teach and train our children in the Word, showing them the love and forgiveness of the Father as new creations in Christ. Fighting for your blended family takes courage, patience, and perseverance. And a whole lot of faith! But you don't do it alone. God is on your side to see you through the challenges (see Luke 1:37).

Scripture Reading

This explains why a man leaves his father and mother and is joined to his wife, and the two are united into one (Genesis 2:24, NLT).

Love [*agape*] your neighbor as yourself (Matthew 22:39 NLT).

For with God nothing will be impossible (Luke 1:37).

Discussion Questions

1. Why can putting children first actually jeopardize blended families?

2. According to the law of partnership, how can blended family members build trust and unity?

3. How should discipline be handled in a blended family?

Reflection Questions

1. How might your priorities need to shift to put your marriage at the center if you are in a blended family?

2. What fears may be influencing your parenting decisions in your blended family?

3. How can you build greater trust and unity with your spouse around parenting decisions?

Connect with the Father

Dear Father, thank You for always being by my side no matter what. Thank You for Your strength to fight for my family and to fight for a strong relationship with my spouse. Help us to create a stable home for our children so that they may praise Your name. In Jesus' name, Amen.

Until Next Time …

- Read Chapter 13: Be the First
- Ask the Lord, "What do You want me to learn from this chapter?"

Chapter 13 Guide

Be the First

Recap

- Equally as important as the law of priority is the law of partnership—the melding of two people into one.

- When remarrying, the new spouse should not be made less important than the children.

- Courtesy and love (*agape*) must be shown to the children of a new spouse.

The Big Idea

Your past and your family history do not have to define you. By living for God, you can be the first in your family to break negative generational cycles and bring healing for your future generations.

Chapter Review

The hardest place to be in a battle is on the front lines. If you're the first generation to raise your children according to biblical principles, it's going to be difficult. But the trials are worth it when you pass a different inheritance onto your children.

Whatever your family history, broken relationships don't have to define you. And they definitely don't have to define your relationship with Jesus. Whether your parents struggled with addictions or put work before family, you can and will be healed by the blood of Jesus. Through Him, the rejection, the hurtful put-downs, and the domineering personalities will no longer hold you captive. Instead, He will empower you to walk in freedom.

Every parent needs to think about the generational effects of their behavior. The present is not the only thing that matters. Godly parents want to see God's generational blessing on their family so that their children have the advantage in life. This means serving the Lord in your own life regardless of what your parents may think of your faith. Your children need two things to thrive: God and you. Everything else will fall into place from there.

It is better to build your house on the Rock than on the sand (see Matthew 7:24–27). At the beach, the sand is more popular than the rocks because sand is more comfortable and more conformable. When you lie in the sand, you leave your imprint on it. When you lie on a rock, it leaves its imprint on you. Jesus is the Rock. He isn't going to conform to what you want. Rather, we conform to Him. He is the Son of God, and we are His disciples.

We're currently living in an *anti*-biblical culture where custom-made Christianity is all the rage. But we can't pick and choose. Either we accept Jesus for who He is, or we reject Him. There are no other options.

If you're living on the Rock, Jesus promises two things: you will be persecuted by the world, and you will have total security. You may lose friends and relationships, but you will live with divine peace when your life is built on the Rock.

Many people believe what the Bible says but build their lives on the sand anyway because they think that a godly life is too hard. But the point of being a Christian is doing the hard things no one else is willing to do. Having a rock beneath may be uncomfortable, but it is stable. Your life will be peaceful while everyone else's is falling apart. Your children and your grandchildren will stand while other people fall.

And if you raise your children on the Word of God, you will have no regrets. It is a stable foundation because Jesus is the same yesterday, today, and forever (Hebrews 13:8). If you were raised in a Christian family, you may not be able to relate. But if you're the first Christian in your family, well done. Be strong in the Lord. It takes courage to be the first, but it will turn out to be the best decision you ever made.

Scripture Reading

"Therefore whoever hears these sayings of Mine, and does them, I will liken him to a wise man who built his house on the rock: and the rain descended, the floods came, and the winds blew and beat on that house; and it did not fall, for it was founded on the rock.

But everyone who hears these sayings of Mine, and does not do them, will be like a foolish man who built his house on the sand: and the rain descended, the floods came, and the winds blew and beat on that house; and it fell. And great was its fall" (Matthew 7:24–27).

Your word *is* a lamp to my feet
And a light to my path (Psalm 119:105).

"But seek first the kingdom of God and His righteousness, and all these things shall be added to you" (Matthew 6:33).

Discussion Questions

1. How can spouses support and encourage each other in building their lives on the Rock? How can they pray for and challenge one another?

2. Why do you think dysfunctional patterns get passed down through generations?

3. How can being part of a loving Christian community help heal generational brokenness and pain?

Reflection Questions

1. What generational cycles have shaped your family? What should be kept? What should be changed?

2. Have you had experiences where sticking to biblical principles was uncomfortable but proved worthwhile?

3. Where have you already seen God's faithfulness or blessing in your family, despite generational brokenness?

Connect with the Father

Dear Father, thank You for being my Father. Your love, Your presence, and Your Word are the most important things in my life. Bless my parents—I know they did the best they could, given their circumstances. Help me to live a life that is completely dedicated to You. Make me more like You. In Jesus' name, Amen.

Until Next Time …

- Read Chapter 14: Gatekeeper
- Ask the Lord, "What do You want me to learn from this chapter?"

Chapter 14 Guide

Gatekeeper

Recap

- Being the first generation to live for God is difficult but worth it.

- When you live on the Rock (Jesus), you will be:

  o Persecuted by the world.
  o Have total security.

The Big Idea

Jesus has given us the authority to lock up (bind) the power of the enemy and to unlock (loose) the power of the kingdom of heaven. Parents are the gatekeepers for their children's lives.

Chapter Review

The first time Jesus mentions the Church, He tells Peter that whatever gates he locks on earth will be locked in heaven, and whatever he unlocks on earth will be unlocked in heaven (see Matthew 16:18–19). In other words, Jesus was telling Peter that he was a gatekeeper. And so are you.

Adam and Eve were the first gatekeepers on earth, but they opened the wrong door, allowing Satan's temptation to influence them and wreak havoc. In Matthew 16, Jesus returns the keys of earth (and the kingdom of heaven) to believers. We have total authority over all the power of the enemy. As long as you use the keys in your hand against him, the devil can't harm you. He would kill you if he had the chance! But because of Jesus, the devil has no authority over your life.

As a gatekeeper under God, there are seven gates to your life that must be guarded well:

1. **Eyes** – What do you allow yourself and your kids to watch or read? What do you look at on the internet?

2. **Ears** – What music and podcasts do you listen to? What kind of language do your friends, family, and coworkers use around you?

3. **Mouth** – What words do you speak over yourself and others? How do you respond to

rumors and gossip? How often do you worship and pray?

4. **Mind** – What thoughts do you focus on? What do you allow yourself to daydream about? What beliefs do you actively try to build up or tear down?

5. **Spirit** – Do you live in rebellion and unbelief? Have you received salvation by grace through faith? Is Jesus the Lord and Savior of your life?

6. **Flesh** – When you want something, whom do you ask for help? What physical needs demand your attention? Whom do you trust to meet your sexual desires?

7. **Emotion** – What are the biggest temptations you face? How do you respond when bad things happen? Do your feelings dictate your attitude?

As the gatekeeper, you decide what you let in and what you keep out. We all are responsible for the gates of our lives. Not your parents or friends—*you*. Whatever is in your life, you have allowed it to be there.

As a parent, you are the gatekeeper of your home. That is not your kids' responsibility. The devil is just waiting for a gate to be left open in a child's life. Here are four gates in a child's life that a parent must guard:

- **God** – God is the most important gate in your child's life. As the parent, it is your responsibility to teach your child the love of God and the truth of His Word at the earliest age possible. The moment they accept Jesus as the Lord of their life, your job is to disciple them in their faith so that they can bear the image of God. Discipleship includes taking your child to church, reading the Bible to them, praying with them, etc. Being in a church is very important because all Christians need community. When we are surrounded by other believers, we hold each other accountable, encourage each other, and fight alongside each other. Being a solo Christian quickly leads to problems. It's better to live in a pack.

- **Friends** – There is a balance when it comes to whom you allow to be around your child. Caution is always good, but it should never turn into legalism. Legalism always produces rebellion because it is based on rules and not relationship. You can't prevent your child from interacting with other kids, especially while they're at school. But you can teach them how to recognize good friends from bad ones and how to love everyone while standing up for their beliefs. God will give you wisdom when your child needs to be removed from a situation. And if that does need to happen, open and honest communication is key. Remember to thank your child for trusting you and have a conversation with them—not a lecture—so that they can understand why you're doing what you're doing.

- **Entertainment** – Technology is nearly unavoidable in today's world. It's easy to give a kid a tablet and let them keep themselves occupied. And with devices all around the house, it can be easy to become too lenient about what we allow them to do online. Not everything on the internet is bad, but not all of it is good either. Thankfully there are some great parent control programs designed to keep children safe online. We recommend finding the best one and installing it on every device. You cannot give your child access to an electronic instrument that you are unwilling to monitor.

- **Education** – Yes, parents even have authority to educate their children. This doesn't necessarily mean homeschooling your child, but it does mean staying involved in their education. Do you know what your child is learning? Does it align with Christian values, or is the Bible attacked in the classroom? School is no longer simply about learning reading, writing, and arithmetic. There are subtle philosophies and mindsets being taught in classes that are unbiblical. Sometimes you will have to have conversations with them about what they learned, and sometimes God may tell you to change their school. Changing schools is not easy, but if that's what God has called you to do, it will be worth it. Even Christian schools aren't perfect, so no matter where you child attends, it's up to you to raise them and guard what they are learning.

When your children are grown, they will be thankful that you guarded them from the enemy. And they will become responsible gatekeepers themselves.

Scripture Reading

Behold, I give you the authority to trample on serpents and scorpions, and over all the power of the enemy, and nothing shall by any means hurt you (Luke 10:19).

Death and life *are* in the power of the tongue,
And those who love it will eat its fruit
(Proverbs 18:21).

For the weapons of our warfare *are* not carnal but mighty in God for pulling down strongholds, casting down arguments and every high thing that exalts itself against the knowledge of God, bringing every thought into captivity to the obedience of Christ (2 Corinthians 10:4–5).

For we do not have a High Priest who cannot sympathize with our weaknesses, but was in all *points* tempted as *we are, yet* without sin (Hebrews 4:15).

Do not be misled: "Bad company corrupts good character" (1 Corinthians 15:33 NIV).

Discussion Questions

1. What boundaries and guidelines can be put in place to guard your children's gates?

2. What are some practical ways parents can lead their children to know God from an early age?

3. How can parents teach their kids to choose good friends? What are signs of a potentially bad influence?

Reflection Questions

1. How do you balance showing your child trust while still protecting them from negative influences?

2. Are there ways you may have been legalistic in your parenting? How can you parent through having a relationship with your kids?

3. Is your child's relationship with God the top priority in your home?

Connect with the Father

Dear Father, help me to be a responsible gatekeeper over my own life and over the lives of my children. Give me wisdom so that I may know what to let in and what to keep out. Guard my children's hearts and minds while they are at school or with friends. And help me to guide them in love rather than from fear. In Jesus' name, Amen.

Until Next Time …

- Read Chapter 15: Training Maneuvers
- Ask the Lord, "What do You want me to learn from this chapter?"

Chapter 15 Guide

Training Maneuvers

Recap

- You are the gatekeeper of your own life, and you must watch over these gates:

  o Eyes
  o Ears
  o Mouth
  o Mind
  o Spirit
  o Flesh
  o Emotion

- You are also the gatekeeper of your children's lives, and you must carefully monitor these gates:

  o God
  o Friends
  o Entertainment
  o Education

The Big Idea

There will be seasons when your child is tempted to make bad decisions. When that happens, hold onto God's promise that you will see them return to righteousness.

Chapter Review

Did you know every promise of God is conditional upon some act of obedience on your part? In the case of raising children, the condition is *training* them. Then, when they are old, they will not depart from God (Proverbs 22:6). Children need their parents to show them what to do, not just tell them. After all, "a picture paints a thousand words." Raising is not the same as training. Raising only means to grow something. That would mean only feeding, clothing, and protecting your child until they are physically mature. Training them is showing them how to live in the kingdom of God.

Modeling godly behavior is essential to training a child. Be careful of practicing the saying, "Do as we say, not as we do!" Children can recognize that hypocrisy. You will break your child's spirit if you expect them to do something that you're not doing (or not willing to do) yourself. Modeling means showing them how it's done. You can tell them off all day, but letting them see you do what you ask them to do will go much farther. We can't expect our children to do things the right way when we've never shown them how.

Whether you like it or not, your children will grow up to be like you, just like you grew up the way your parents' behavior taught you. Even how you treat your spouse in front of the children teaches them what to expect in marriage and how to treat their future spouse. Your behavior is the greatest influence on your children. And a godly parent isn't afraid of replicating themselves in their kids. You'll still make mistakes. But if you do, the best thing to do is to be open with your children and repent of that bad example to them, to God, and to your spouse. Kick that area from your life!

Training your child means communicating to them God's love, His Word, and His principles for living from the time they're born to the time they leave your house. The amount of time you spend with your child is crucial. Yet many parents spend just as much time on their phones (or occupied with other technology) as they do with their kids. Keep technology as a tool, not a priority. Your children are more important. Are you willing to spend thousands and thousands of hours with them? You may be wondering, *What could you possibly talk about with your children for that long?* That's the time to talk about the Bible and about your expectations. That's the time to answer their questions about God and the situations they've been facing. It's okay if you don't have all the answers. If you don't know something, go find the answer. Train your children well.

Accountability is crucial in communication. Once a standard of behavior has been given to a child, it is important to hold them (and yourself) to that standard. Find what God's Word says about good behavior and explain it to them. If they do something bad, they should be disciplined; if they do something good, they should be rewarded. This can begin at a very young age. Even something as simple as making sure they obey you when you tell them to clean up their toys is important. Children who aren't held accountable don't understand the weight of their actions, and they grow into reckless teenagers and irresponsible adults.

As we train our children, we must give them grace as they learn right from wrong. That is why we reward them for doing right just as we discipline them for doing something wrong. Remember, once you make a commitment on how to reward or discipline, you must be consistent in administering it. Never promise something you can't or don't intend to keep. Why? Because God our Father is consistent. He is a loving disciplinarian when we do something wrong, and He is a loving rewarder when we do something right.

Scripture Reading

Train up a child in the way he should go,
And when he is old he will not depart from it
(Proverbs 22:6).

The righteous *man* walks in his integrity;
His children *are* blessed after him (Proverbs 20:7).

How can a young man keep his way pure?
By keeping *it* according to Your word
(Psalm 119:9 NASB).

Discussion Questions

1. Why is living by example more powerful than just telling kids what to do?

2. Why is following through on consequences and rewards critical? How does this reflect God's character?

3. Why is it important to hold children accountable to the standards set for them?

4. How can parents give grace while training their children?

Reflection Questions

1. Are you raising or training your children? Why is this difference important? How can you train your children?

2. How much quality time are you investing in training your kids each day? What can you do to increase meaningful interactions?

3. Have you established clear rewards and consequences for good and bad behavior? How are you being consistent with this?

Connect with the Father

Dear Father, we thank You for this Word and this promise about training our children. Reveal to us any issue that would cause us not to have the right resources for parenting and heal the pain and hurt caused by these issues. We resolve that we are not going to be bullied by a fallen world, to reject Your Word, or to believe in anything other than Your promises. Your Word is eternal, and it is powerful. Your Word has a guarantee that it will not return void, and we want to be good models to our children. We are committed to train up our children in the way You want them to go. May blessings flow upon our home. In Jesus' name, Amen.

Until Next Time …

- Read Chapter 16: The War of Words

- Ask the Lord, "What do You want me to learn from this chapter?"

BATTLEFIELDS

Communication
Discipline
and
Sexuality

The War for Words

Recap

- Training a child means teaching them how to live a godly life:

  - o By being a good example through your own words and actions.
  - o By communicating with your children as often as you can about God and the truth.
  - o By showing them grace as they learn right from wrong.

- Once you've set a standard or expectation, stick to it.

The Big Idea

Words have power. We must be aware of how we use them with our children. As parents, we must be intentional about speaking life and blessing into our kids.

Chapter Review

How we speak to our children is very important. Children need an abundance of positive and truthful words, but the enemy will do everything he can to distort our words to poison our children. Our children's future hangs in the balance of who wins the war for our words.

Our words have far more power than we can imagine. They can build up or tear down, encourage or discourage. There are no such things as neutral words. Whatever words you "sow" into your children will determine the harvest that you reap from them (Proverbs 18:21). If you sow positive words, you will reap positive results. If you sow negative words, you will reap negative results. Therefore, every word you speak to your children should contain praise, kindness, or the truth in love.

When we seek God's presence and approach His throne, the first order of business is to praise Him, no matter how we may be feeling in the moment. By faith, we pour out a sacrifice of thanksgiving and praise to our Father and lay aside any negative, complaining spirits. We are created in the image of God, and we are His temple. When we praise the Lord, He cleanses us of our pains and negative feelings. But if we insist on griping and complaining, then the Lord can't move, because our eyes are not on Him. This leads to spiritual death.

In a similar way, when we only see the things our children don't do right and we use our words to put them down because of those mistakes, we completely lose our influence with our children. They quickly close their hearts when they are addressed with a critical tone. They may comply with your desire in that moment, but the hurt that your words brought will plant the seeds of rebellion in them.

Instead of digging in the dirt to find things wrong with them, start looking for gold and praise the things they do right. Say things like, "You are so smart!" and "Good job! I knew you could do it!" Find what they do right and praise it, praise it, praise it! When you praise your child, they are drawn to you and want to be around you.

Your children will want to be around whoever praises them. If you're not praising them, someone else—who may or may not be a good influence—will, and they will be the ones speaking into your children's lives. So keep praising your children. When you praise them, you earn the right to correct them.

Kindness is a fruit of the Spirit. It means that you respect the high value and emotions of the person to whom you're speaking. When we talk down to a person, we are no longer showing that we value that person. God values you highly. He also highly values your children. When the Father's love for you sinks into your soul, you will want to control your emotions. You will want to find the right words to speak, the right tone to use, the right facial expressions to show. This means not using rude words and gestures. Those are not kind.

Showing unkindness to our children teaches them that they are not valuable, and they'll begin to think and act like they're not valuable. They'll become cynical and untrusting of others. They will not value their own lives or the lives of others, leading to suicidal thoughts and attempts.

None of us are perfect parents, and most (if not all) of us have said things in anger to our children that have wounded them. When this happens, we should admit that we've messed up and apologize for hurting them. Being open like that with your children teaches them how to handle conflict and emotions in a healthy manner without fear.

Every successful relationship must be balanced with truth and love. When we speak truth, we set a standard for our children (and for ourselves) and prevent moral degradation. But truth spoken without love is harsh and cruel and never produces anything positive. On the other hand, love values the other person and creates a connection. But love without truth is spineless and weak. We need both to maintain a healthy balance. Consider:

- Relationships of truth without love dry up.

- Relationships of love without truth blow up.

- Relationships of truth and love grow up.

When applying truth to your children, always keep an atmosphere of love. They will always respect you for it.

Some of you are still hurting from a word spoken over you years ago. That word created feelings of self-hate or low self-esteem. Know that Jesus is full of grace and truth, and He cares for you. He loves you unconditionally. You are loved. Let that love overflow out of you to your children. Just as God's love draws you to Him, let your love draw your family closer together. Then your family will be invincible and eternal.

Scripture Reading

Pleasant words *are like* a honeycomb,
Sweetness to the soul and health to the bones
(Proverbs 16:24).

There is one who speaks like the piercings of a sword,
But the tongue of the wise *promotes* health
(Proverbs 12:18).

Enter into His gates with thanksgiving,
And into His courts with praise.
Be thankful to Him, *and* bless His name
(Psalm 100:4).

But, speaking the truth in love, may grow up in all things into Him who is the head—Christ (Ephesians 4:15).

Discussion Questions

1. How can the hurt from words linger for years and affect how people see themselves?

2. Why is praise so important for reaching a child's heart? How can parents praise their kids even in the midst of conflict?

3. How can we monitor and control our tone of voice, facial expressions, and body language when engaging with our kids?

Reflection Questions

1. How can you be more intentional about using words to bless your children rather than tear them down? What practical steps can you take?

2. Have negative words shaped how you see yourself? How can you break free and embrace God's view of yourself?

3. How do you want your speech and communication to reflect the heart of God for your child in the days ahead?

Connect with the Father

Dear Father, I give You praise. Thank You for Your love and grace over my life. Help me to show that same love and grace to my spouse and to my children. Let the words of my mouth and the thoughts of my heart be acceptable to You. Help me encourage my children. Give them Your abundant life. In Jesus' name, Amen.

Until Next Time ...

- Read Chapter 17: Communication Challenges
- Ask the Lord, "What do You want me to learn from this chapter?"

Chapter 17 Guide

Communication Challenges

Recap

- Our words bring either life or death to our children. Let's make sure that it's always life.

- When speaking with your children, make sure your words fall into one of these categories:

  o Praise
  o Kindness
  o Speaking truth in love.

The Big Idea

Communication is key! Poor communication creates dysfunctional families, but good communication helps overcome more problems than you'd think.

Chapter Review

Children learn how to talk from their parents and family members. More than studying how to make sounds and string them together to speak your language, children watch their parents to learn how to communicate ideas and feelings. If you bottle up your emotions until you explode, your kids will copy that. If you speak everything that's on your mind with no filter, your kids will copy that too.

Perhaps your parents were poor communicators. Once you recognize that negative trait in their lives, you may see it in your life too. That's the time to break the generational cycle over you as we mentioned a few chapters before.

Everyone's personality is different. They have positive and negative traits. Spouses with different personalities will struggle to communicate if they expect the other person to speak their emotional language. They must take the time to listen and to learn how to speak to one another. Most importantly, they must learn how to communicate in an open, honest, and loving manner.

It's the same with your children. Your children may be similar to you, but they may also have their own personalities. Perhaps their personality is more similar to your spouse's than yours. Either way, we must learn to adapt and communicate with each child in the way that will be most effective for them. Without taking the time to understand how they think and communicate, you will become frustrated and may take out your frustration on your child verbally. When you do that, you send a message to your kids that parents are harsh and cruel. Their picture of God will become warped. They will see Him as a dictator who doesn't really care for them. Or else they will see Him as unpredictable or even schizophrenic, someone who loves them one minute and hates them the next.

But God loves His children. His mercies are new every morning. If your relationship with your child feels shaky, approach them in love, with understanding and with openness.

Discipline issues should always be resolved in a timely manner so that your heart doesn't harden toward your kids. When you go to bed angry at your children (or at anybody), you allow that anger to settle into your subconscious and become a part of you. Don't wait! No matter what form of discipline you choose, you need to apply it and forgive the child right then. When Jesus said to forgive someone seventy-times-seven times, the majority of those times will be used for your child (see Matthew 18:22).

Every act of correction and discipline must come from a place of relationship. When discipline is doled out because you've had a bad day, it emphasizes the rules but harms the relationship, creating a rebellious spirit in your child.

Discipline takes patience. You won't always see immediate results. In fact, most of the time you probably won't. But if you discipline expecting your child to change right then and there, you'll break their spirit.

Discipline takes faith. Sometimes you may feel like you're correcting the same issue over and over again. You may wonder if your child will ever grow out of it. But you are planting seeds for the future. Stick to the standards you have put in place. Believe that what you are doing for your child now will eventually pay off in the future. You may not see it until your children are in college or well into adulthood. But God is faithful, and you will see the fruit of your labor.

Scripture Reading

My dear brothers and sisters, take note of this: Everyone should be quick to listen, slow to speak and slow to become angry (James 1:19 NIV).

Through the LORD'S mercies we are not consumed, Because His compassions fail not.
They are new every morning;
Great *is* Your faithfulness (Lamentations 3:22–23).

"Be angry, and do not sin": do not let the sun go down on your wrath (Ephesians 4:26).

Discussion Questions

1. What are some examples of poor communication within a family? How do those examples negatively impact relationships?

2. How can parents adapt their communication style to the unique personality of each child? How could this be beneficial?

3. How can parents make sure that their relationship with their kids is never sacrificed for the sake of discipline?

Reflection Questions

1. How can you adapt your communication style to connect better with each unique child?

2. When have you gone to bed angry at your child? What was the result? How can you avoid this in the future?

3. What are your strengths and weaknesses when it comes to communicating with your family? How can you build on your strengths and recognize your weaknesses in order to communicate more effectively?

Connect with the Father

Dear Father, teach me how to communicate according to Your Word. Give me patience with my spouse and with my children. Help me to understand their personalities so that I can talk with them effectively. And give me wisdom on how to discipline properly, with love and without harshness. In Jesus' name, Amen.

Until Next Time …

- Read Chapter 18: The Discipline Battle
- Ask the Lord, "What do You want me to learn from this chapter?"

Chapter 18 Guide

The Discipline Battle

Recap

- Children learn how to communicate from their parents and family members.

- Different personalities can clash, but practicing understanding improves communication.

- Discipline must be firm, but it should never be done in anger.

- Discipline requires patience and faith.

The Big Idea

As the world turns darker, parents need to be a light to their children. They need to know they are loved. Loving discipline is one way to show them that they are loved.

Chapter Review

As the traditional view on marriage is displaced more and more, families face more temptations and social obstacles concerning sexuality and sexual activity. Our only yet our greatest defense is parenting from God's Word. Scripturally, family crises can be avoided through loving discipline in the home.

Loving discipline—and yes, that includes spanking done the right way—tells a child that they are loved (see Proverbs 13:24). And a disciplined child brings peace and rest and will be a delight to their parents. A child who is not disciplined brings anxiety and stress. What you do now will be reflected later in their lives.

While we believe spanking should be used as a form of discipline, this does not mean that we condone child abuse. Abuse subjects the child to harmful physical, emotional, or spiritual influences that demonstrate something to them that is not in God's nature. But proper spanking protects the child, helps them see that there are consequences in life for bad behavior, and teaches them that God punishes those who disobey Him and His Word.

A proper spanking scenario would go something like this: You warned your son, Johnny, concerning something. Johnny is old enough to understand your expectations. You have warned him that if he continues to disobey, he will be spanked. Then he disobeys again. You take him to a private area—never discipline your child in public. And never scream or shout out in anger.

When you get there, you calmly explain to Johnny how he has just disobeyed you, and you tell him that he will now be spanked. Johnny may be crying, begging, bargaining, or twisting around. But you should keep a straight face and control your emotions. Use a paddle, wooden spoon, or wooden rod (never your hand or a random instrument) and swat the child on the bottom hard enough to cause discomfort but not hard enough to cause damage.

When you finish the spanking, sit down with Johnny and hug him. Tell him you love him and forgive him, and you do not want him to disobey you anymore. Pray for him. When you finish, you say, "Johnny, I love you. You are a very good boy. Now, go and have fun!"

Always follow through with the spanking after your first warning. When a parent doesn't follow through, the child learns that your word means nothing and will continue to misbehave until your emotions are out of control. God does not act in this way. When He says He will do something, He will do it every time. He gains your faith through His faithfulness. As a parent, you are to be the same way.

Biblical discipline is *never* abusive. It does not include making marks and bruises on your child's body. It does not create fear in the child through lies, such as "God is going to get you for that!" or "If you do that, your eyes will fall out of your head!" Biblical discipline is loving and comes from wanting the child to grow into the best person they can be in Christ.

In the past several decades, "experts" in child-rearing methods have said that spanking causes children to resent and hate their parents and encourages them to adopt violent lifestyles. But this is a fad philosophy based on the current views of society. Such philosophies are always changing. For example, years ago, "experts" discouraged mothers from nursing their babies and said that formula was healthier. Then it changed again, and they said that breastmilk was healthier.

These experts, aside from giving inconsistent philosophies, directly contradict God's Word, which promotes properly done spanking as a form of discipline (see again Proverbs 13:24).

The basis for the anti-spanking movement is humanism, which says that humans do not have a sin nature. According to humanism, everyone is inherently good, and evil is learned as the child grows up. But if children are inherently good, then why are they naturally selfish and rebellious? Why do they cry if a toy is rightly taken from them or when they don't get their way? It is because all of us are born with a sinful nature, contrary to God and, therefore, contrary to good behavior. The Holy Spirit produces the good fruit within us once we begin to follow Jesus (Galatians 5:22). Without Him, we are not truly good, and we cannot be saved by our own goodness.

Contrary to the "experts," spanking does not make a child violent. Abuse does that. Correct discipline teaches a child respect for others and how to control their behavior.

Spanking is not always the answer. Sometimes a child is acting out because they have some unmet need or hurt. A parent must be sensitive to the differences in behaviors and open to the Holy Spirit to help them discern the root of the problem. Though grounding tends to punish the parents along with the child, sometimes it may be necessary, along with the withdrawal of certain privileges, added responsibilities, and other methods that do not damage the child or subject them to an ungodly influence.

Most important of all, parents must agree on what forms of discipline to use. Neither parent should be the sole disciplinarian. This creates an unhealthy "good cop/bad cop" scenario that puts tension on the child's relationship with one parent while the other appears to be doting. Both parents should discipline and show affection. Your child desperately needs you both to guide them through life, to teach them, and to love them.

Scripture Reading

Whoever spares the rod hates their children,
but the one who loves their children is careful to
discipline them (Proverbs 13:24 NIV).

A rod and a reprimand impart wisdom,
but a child left undisciplined disgraces its mother
(Proverbs 29:15 NIV).

Correct your son, and he will give you rest;
Yes, he will give delight to your soul
(Proverbs 29:17).

Now no chastening seems to be joyful for the present, but painful; nevertheless, afterward it yields the peaceable fruit of righteousness to those who have been trained by it (Hebrews 12:11).

Discussion Questions

1. When is spanking not the right disciplinary tactic to use? What are some alternative forms of discipline?

2. How could differing approaches to discipline from parents confuse children or undermine parental authority?

3. How is discipline connected to expressing love and care for children?

Reflection Questions

1. Do you believe spanking is an appropriate form of discipline? Why or why not? What guidelines do you suggest?

2. How would you handle disciplining your child if your spouse disagreed with your methods? What compromise could you reach?

3. When is it appropriate to use alternative forms of discipline instead of spanking? What factors should guide that decision?

4. If spanking is one of your methods of discipline, how can you mentally and emotionally prepare yourself to spank your child in a calm, controlled manner?

Connect with the Father

Dear Father, thank You for disciplining me lovingly. Help me to do the same for my children. Help me never to lash out in anger but to stay in control of my emotions. Give me wisdom in each scenario so that I can discipline my children properly and not harshly or without understanding. Help my children to understand that I love them just as You love them. In Jesus' name, Amen.

Until Next Time …

- Read Chapter 19: The Purpose of Discipline
- Ask the Lord, "What do You want me to learn from this chapter?"

Chapter 19 Guide

The Purpose of Discipline

Recap

- Loving discipline shows your children that you love them.

- Your anger or the child's misbehavior does not give you the right to verbally or physically abuse them.

- Biblical discipline is never abusive because God is not abusive.

- Spanking should not be the cure-all for every problem.

- No matter what, parents must always be in agreement about how to discipline the child.

The Big Idea

Disciplining your child should never be done without thought. It has great importance in shaping them into who God has created them to be.

Chapter Review

The purpose of biblical child discipline is fourfold.

First, it serves to protect them from their sin nature. We must protect our children because they are not able to do it themselves. Sin is inherent; good behavior is not. Good behavior must be taught. Children do not understand that sin is dangerous, and they also don't know that there are always consequences to their behavior, whether good or bad. If they learn to forgive someone, their hearts are kept pure. If they touch a hot stove, they will be burned.

Discipline protects them from their foolish and sinful nature and helps them live up to their full potential. Disciplining them when they are young over little things like not picking up fragile dangerous objects to play with teaches them to listen to your voice. When you speak, you are looking out for their best interests. It trains them to stop the moment you say "Stop!" It may even save their lives.

Second, biblical discipline instills character and moral values. It is important to train children to respect others and authority. Since society hardly allows teachers to discipline anymore, it is up to you as the parent to teach your children to respect their teachers. Naturally, they should not submit to immoral teachers, but they should be able to respond appropriately to good authority.

Truthfulness is another important moral value. Lying is of the devil, the father of lies (John 8:44), and he will try to lure God's children into trouble by lying. Even what might be considered "little white lies" are dangerous and need to be addressed. As the parents, make sure not to send mixed messages to your children. Live by example. When you punish your child for lying, make sure you don't lie to others.

A strong work ethic is also a positive trait to instill into your children. You don't have to be a slave driver to show them the importance of doing good work with a cheerful attitude.

The third purpose of biblical discipline is to prepare your children for reality and success. They are not so special that they can get away with anything. If they do something wrong, they will be punished. But when they learn right from wrong and choose right, then their lives will be wonderful, and they will live successfully.

When you take your children out in public, that's the time to teach them to respect other people's property. When you go out into the real world, your restraint is tested. And sinful desires have a very loud voice. But if they give into those sinful desires, the world will discipline them severely. Your discipline will be more gracious and more effective because yours is coming from a place of love.

Finally, biblical discipline helps children understand and accept God. Parents are the first image of God that children ever see. And God is a disciplinarian because He loves us. He has standards while being merciful.

The majority of "Christians" in America today do not believe that truth is absolute, which means that right and wrong would only be based on one's perception of what is right or wrong. In other words, anything goes. But that is not reality. Despite what our culture says, there is truth that needs to be taught. And the best way you can teach it is through your own behavior. A parent's behavior has more power and influence on a child's concept of God than anything else. A godly parent is an authority figure who is extremely loving and kind and involved in their child's life *and* someone who means what they say. This is a difficult task. *Parenting* is a difficult task. But God knew that. That's why He gave us His Word and His Holy Spirit to help us. Godly discipline will make a difference in the lives of your children, both now and for eternity.

Scripture Reading

My son, do not make light of the Lord's discipline,
and do not lose heart when he rebukes you,
because the Lord disciplines the one he loves,
and he chastens everyone he accepts as his son
(Hebrews 12:5–6 NIV).

Foolishness *is* bound up in the heart of a child;
The rod of correction will drive it far from him
(Proverbs 22:15).

Chasten your son while there is hope,
And do not set your heart on his destruction
(Proverbs 19:18).

Discussion Questions

1. Why is it important for parents to discipline their children? What purposes does it serve?

2. How can discipline prepare children for success in the real world? What lessons does it teach them?

3. How can parents model integrity and godly behavior when disciplining their kids? What hypocrisies must be avoided?

4. What character traits and moral values should parents seek to instill through discipline?

Reflection Questions

1. Do I explain the reasons behind my discipline so my children understand that I have their best interests in mind?

2. Do I follow through consistently on discipline and consequences? Where can I improve?

3. What practical steps can I take to make discipline more effective and purposeful in my home?

Connect with the Father

Dear Father, thank You for guiding my life. Continue to lead me and teach me right from wrong. Thank You that Your Word is absolute Truth and that I can build my life upon it. Help me to discipline my children properly according to Your Truth so that they may grow up to be lights in this world. In Jesus' name, Amen.

Until Next Time …

- Read Chapter 20: Discipline Strategies, Part 1

- Ask the Lord, "What do You want me to learn from this chapter?"

Discipline Strategies, Part 1

Recap

- Biblical discipline is fourfold:

  o To protect children from their sin nature.
  o To instill character and moral values.
  o To prepare them for reality and success.
  o To help them understand and accept God.

- God has given us His Word and His Holy Spirit to help us live well and raise our children properly.

The Big Idea

Effective discipline teaches children to respond promptly to parents' instruction, just as God acts decisively when people disobey Him. Parents can discipline effectively by using clarity and consistency.

Chapter Review

The next two chapters will answer the "how to" questions of parenting through the four Cs of discipline.

Clarity is the ability to communicate clearly and in a relational manner when disciplining your children. How old they are will determine how this looks. Little ones from birth to three or four years old must be trained to respond to your voice commands. When little Johnny is reaching for a hot stove, your immediate instinct should be to say, "Don't touch that." You won't take the time to explain why. There isn't time! Once Johnny is safely away from the stove, then you can explain what "hot" means. But in the moment of reaching for the stove, they will not understand a long-winded explanation. They *will* understand, "Don't touch that, or you'll get a spanking."

As children mature, it will be important to explain to them the consequences of their actions. Don't ever discipline your children for something they don't understand. Explain the rules and consequences to them clearly. Then have them repeat it back to make sure that they were listening and understand what you have said. This saves you from the most infamous tactic, "I didn't hear what you said."

Honoring each other within the household is so important. This can be taught through godly discipline and with the understanding that dishonoring someone has negative consequences.

Consistency is following through with discipline every time a child violates the rule. Inconsistency is the number one cause of a child not obeying their parents. It's fruitless to repeat over and over, "Maddie, don't do that. Maddie, I'm not going to warn you anymore. Maddie, if you do that one more time. Maddie!" Kids learn the system quickly and will use it to their advantage. If you never follow through with discipline consistently, they will think to themselves, *I can get away with this. I've got about four more warnings left before they do anything.* Then, one day you have a short fuse and take it out on your child after three warnings instead of ten. Now your child is confused and can't figure out why Mom or Dad went crazy.

If you want obedient, well-mannered children, you must discipline with consistency. Give them the rule, then maintain that rule every time. Tell your child to do something in a calm, loving tone. They will not respect your begging and pleading. They must know that when you say something, they are to listen immediately or there will be consequences. And they must learn it early in life.

Scripture Reading

But let your 'Yes' be 'Yes,' and your 'No,' 'No.' For whatever is more than these is from the evil one (Matthew 5:37).

Do not be deceived, God is not mocked; for whatever a man sows, that he will also reap (Galatians 6:7).

And let us not grow weary while doing good, for in due season we shall reap if we do not lose heart (Galatians 6:9).

Discussion Questions

1. How can parents set clear expectations and consequences for their children's behavior?

2. What are some potential consequences for not enforcing consistent discipline?

3. How can parents help children understand reasons for rules and consequences?

4. How does proper discipline demonstrate God's loving and decisive nature?

Reflection Questions

1. In what ways are you unclear or inconsistent when disciplining your children? How can you improve?

2. How often do you explain the reasons for rules and consequences to your children? How could you do this more effectively?

3. How do you discipline your children? Is it in a calm and loving manner?

Connect with the Father

Dear Father, thank You that You are always the same. I would not understand who You are and who You want me to be otherwise. Help me to parent as You parent. Give me the right words to say to my child so that I can help them understand right from wrong. Help me to be consistent as You are consistent. Thank You that my children are being trained and perfected. In Jesus' name, Amen.

Until Next Time …

- Read Chapter 21: Discipline Strategies, Part 2
- Ask the Lord, "What do You want me to learn from this chapter?"

Chapter 21 Guide

Discipline Strategies, Part 2

Recap

- Always make your rules and consequences clear for your child and speak to them at the level of their understanding.

- Discipline with consistency. Never plead or beg your child; instead, teach them to listen to your voice.

The Big Idea

Effective discipline teaches children to respond promptly to parents' instruction, just as God acts decisively when people disobey Him. Parents can discipline effectively by using correction and compassion.

Chapter Review

The most controversial part of discipline is **correction**. Today's society has been duped by the devil, who has put a twist on the word "discipline." The lack of discipline in our society has created a self-indulgent and rebellious generation. Parents, settle this fact now: God is a disciplinarian, and He expects you to discipline your children according to His Word.

Now we'll talk about the dos and don'ts of discipline. We already talked about spanking—to do it efficiently, without anger, and never with your hands. Grounding is another option, though long-term it will affect the entire family. Make sure that the length of time for the grounding is reasonable.

Here are the don'ts for disciplining:

- Never resort to name-calling.

- Never discipline a child in public; find a private space.

- Never yell at your child—yelling is a good indication you are not in control of your emotions.

- Never resort to extreme consequences, such as "You didn't clean your room, so go sleep in the backyard."

Once again, let's go over the correct way to spank a child:

1. Communicate clearly what the child did wrong.

2. Take them to a private place.

3. Swat the child two or three times on their bottom with an appropriate type of paddle.

4. Give hugs and comfort.

5. Forgive them and pray for them.

The most important factor of discipline is to have **compassion** for your child and have a good relationship with them. Remember that a balance of love and truth is critical for maintaining a relationship. When you raise your children with an equal emphasis on your relationship with them and the rules you expect them to obey, you will see them grow into wholesome, healthy-minded young people.

There may be times when your kids begin to close their heart to you, especially as teenagers. Maybe disciplining them doesn't seem to be working anymore. In those cases, try taking some time to spend with them, to have fun together, to do some things they'd like to do. You might be surprised what some quality time does to help them open up to you again. When you feel your children pulling away from you, run after them. Not to smother them—that'll snuff the joy right out of their lives. Guide them with the light of Jesus shining in your life at all times. Model the love of your heavenly Father to them. If your child goes through a difficult stage, trust in the Lord. He listens to you and cares for you. He knows exactly what you and your children need.

Scripture Reading

Discipline your children, for in that there is hope;
do not be a willing party to their death
(Proverbs 19:18 NIV).

And you, fathers, do not provoke your children to wrath, but bring them up in the training and admonition of the Lord (Ephesians 6:4).

Fathers, do not provoke your children, lest they become discouraged (Colossians 3:21).

Discussion Questions

1. What are your thoughts on the spanking debate from a biblical perspective? Where do you stand and why?

2. Why is not disciplining children in public important? What are ways it can be avoided?

3. How can parents maintain close, fun relationships with kids during their teen years? What boundaries need to be set?

4. What are some alternatives to spanking for older kids?

Reflection Questions

1. Do you feel your childhood discipline was biblical or unbiblical? What would you do differently with your own kids?

2. What boundaries or rules do you have the most trouble enforcing? Why do you think that is?

3. How can you grow in modeling God's compassion, mercy, and forgiveness when you discipline your kids?

Connect with the Father

Dear Father, give me the perfect balance of love and truth. Help me to know when to discipline and when to show grace. Protect my children as they go to school and play with their friends. Give me the right words to say if my children go through a difficult stage. Help me to trust You even when things aren't going the way I planned. Let their lives be for Your glory. In Jesus' name, Amen.

Until Next Time …

- Read Chapter 22: Shameless Sexuality

- Ask the Lord, "What do You want me to learn from this chapter?"

Chapter 22 Guide

Shameless Sexuality

Recap

- A lack of discipline keeps a child from learning how to live in society.

- God expects you to discipline your children according to His Word.

- To have a strong relationship with our children, we need to balance discipline (truth) with compassion (love).

The Big Idea

God created sexuality, and He made it good. Satan attacked sexuality at the Fall, causing shame and corruption.

Chapter Review

Sex can be an uncomfortable topic. Some parents don't know what to say, or they're are afraid to say anything. Maybe you're worried about ruining your child's innocence or don't think they're old enough yet. But if you don't talk to your kids about sex, they'll find out about it for themselves from friends, social media, TV shows, movies, etc. It's far better that they hear from you what God's Word says about sex. In order for you to do that, *you* must know what God says about sex and sexuality in general.

Where did your sexuality come from? Believe it or not, God created it. Three times in Genesis 1:27, the Bible says how God created mankind. Both man and woman reflect God's glory in their masculinity and femininity respectively. Males and females are equal, but we are not interchangeable.

Here's the next radical statement: God only created two genders. Not 68. Not 94. *Two*. Scripture does not differentiate between gender identity and biological sex. They are the same thing. Men are male, and women are female.

This is not to diminish the pain of those who are genuinely confused about their identity and truly believe that they are in the wrong type of body. These people deserve our love, respect, and compassion as much as anyone else. We should never abuse or harass someone who is struggling to find the truth. But the answer to this pain is not self-mutilation through the changing of body parts. You can change or remove genitalia, and you can change your name, but you cannot change your gender. All "fixes" are surface-level and only cause more confusion and pain.

Behind the idea of gender reassignment is the belief that humans are here on this earth by accident, which would mean that gender is only a social construct that can be given to someone incorrectly. This belief insists that there is no God or that He exists but is a bungling idiot who can't even follow the instructions of His own lab experiment.

The truth is, we are fearfully and wonderfully made by God (Psalm 139:13–18). And our God doesn't make mistakes. Gender is not a social construct—it's a *God* construct.

The world wants to teach our children that we can be whatever we want to be so long as we're true to ourselves. It says there are no rules except to do what makes you happy. When you are a follower of Jesus Christ, you give up the right of self-determination in any area of your life, including your sexuality. This is what we need to teach our children—truth from God's Word—so that we can prevent future confusion and pain.

When God created Adam and Eve, they were both naked and not ashamed (Genesis 2;25). There was no shame in who they were. God created them as sexual beings for two reasons: to expand the human race (God's family) and for pleasure in marriage. Sexuality is central to God's purpose for your life. This means that you are a sexual person, and your child is also a sexual person. That is not a bad thing. In fact, it's a very good thing. But we have an enemy, and he does all he can to attack sexuality because that is how God's image is multiplied and because it is pleasurable when done in the confines of marriage.

Immediately after the Fall, Adam and Eve realized that they were naked, and they sewed fig leaves together to hide their genitals from God and from each other (Genesis 3:6–7). Suddenly, sexuality became something shameful. When God walked through the garden, Adam and Eve hid from Him, not simply because they had sinned but also because they were naked after they had sinned (Genesis 3:8–10). They felt that they needed to hide because they were ashamed of their God-given sexuality.

Satan wants us to be ashamed of our God-given sexuality so that we will hide it from God. Sexual shame comes from the enemy. Twisted sexuality comes from the enemy. Satan is crafty, and he will put ideas into people's minds and make them think that they came up with it—that they have suddenly become "enlightened," when really they've got it all wrong. Through the devil's influence, Adam and Eve hid from God. Ironically, when we hide our sexuality from God—in other words, when we don't dare associate it with Him—it becomes something that is truly shameful.

By Genesis 6, the entire world was perverted and sexually corrupted. God regretted His creation because when Satan controls the world sexually, the world cannot accomplish the purposes of God.

Sex doesn't gross God out. He created it. He made it to be something pleasurable for His children. If you feel condemned for your sexuality, that is not from God (see Romans 8:1). When we sin in any area, including sexuality, we are convicted. But guilt and shame are never from God. The fact is, Satan wants to control us and keep us from fulfilling God's purpose in our lives. If he can attack our sexuality, he can succeed.

One way the enemy attacks sexuality is he covers the topic with shame so that we try to hide it from our children. We're not suggesting that you have the full "birds and bees" conversation with your four-year-old child. But if they come to you with sincere questions, it's okay to answer them in a way that is age-appropriate. In fact, you should answer them, because you are the godly influence in their lives contradicting the ungodly influences around them. Sexuality should be a series of ongoing, age-appropriate conversations. Even young children can be taught the correct name of their private body parts. Boys have a penis, a scrotum, and testicles. Girls have a vulva, a vagina, and breasts. Teach your children about body privacy and about not allowing others to touch their private parts (trusted adults like doctors excluded).

Don't wait for your child to become a teenager to have these conversations. Children need to know what will happen during puberty before it hits them. And with today's children going through puberty at earlier ages than previous generations, girls as young as eight need to know about breast development and menstrual cycles. Boys as young as nine need to know about erections. Both genders need to understand the function and purpose of their body parts, and they need reassurance from you (their parent) that this is all a normal part of growing up.

You are the most trustworthy person to talk to your children about sex. They should be able to ask you about *anything* and receive an appropriate yet honest answer. They need open communication from you. Don't make them search the internet for information. They will if they think it's their only option. They will find out more than you ever wanted them to know before they reached adulthood. If they come to you with a question and you don't know how to answer it in an age-appropriate way, it's perfectly okay to say, "Can I have a day to pray about this? I want to give you the right information." Just make sure to get back to them within that time period. And never make them feel ashamed that they asked you a question. Always assure your child that their curiosity is natural. But most importantly, make sure they know that they can come to you with their questions and their struggles.

Scripture Reading

So God created mankind in his own image,
in the image of God he created them;
male and female he created them
(Genesis 1:27 NIV).

For You formed my inward parts;
You covered me in my mother's womb.
I will praise You, for I am fearfully *and* wonderfully made;
Marvelous are Your works,
And *that* my soul knows very well
(Psalm 139:13–14).

Professing to be wise, they became fools, and changed the glory of the incorruptible God into an image made like corruptible man—and birds and four-footed animals and creeping things.

   Therefore God also gave them up to uncleanness, in the lusts of their hearts, to dishonor their bodies among themselves, who exchanged the truth of God for the lie, and worshiped and served the creature rather than the Creator, who is blessed forever. Amen.

   For this reason God gave them up to vile passions. For even their women exchanged the natural use for what is against nature. Likewise also the men, leaving the natural use of the woman, burned in their lust for one another, men with men committing what is shameful, and receiving in themselves the penalty of their error which was due (Romans 1:22–27).

I beseech you therefore, brethren, by the mercies of God, that you present your bodies a living sacrifice, holy, acceptable to God, *which is* your reasonable service. And do not be conformed to this world, but be transformed by the renewing of your mind, that you may prove what *is* that good and acceptable and perfect will of God (Romans 12:1–2).

These commandments that I give you today are to be on your hearts. Impress them on your children. Talk about them when you sit at home and when you walk along the road, when you lie down and when you get up (Deuteronomy 6:6–7 NIV).

Discussion Questions

1. Why is sexuality so central to God's purpose for our lives?

2. Why is it important for parents to teach children the proper names for private body parts from a young age?

3. How has Satan attacked human sexuality over time? How have his tactics intensified or changed today?

Reflection Questions

1. How old were you when you first learned about sex? Do you think starting earlier could have helped you? Why or why not?

2. How has shame affected your view of your own sexuality? What can you do to see your sexuality as God does?

3. When have you avoided a tough question from your child? What can you do to be able to answer tough questions in the future?

Connect with the Father

Dear Father, thank You for my sexuality. Thank You that it is a precious gift from You that I don't have to be ashamed about. Remove any shame I have in this area that is hindering Your purpose in my life. Guide my words when my children ask me questions about sex. Help me answer in a way that they can understand and that will protect them from sexual corruption. In Jesus' name, Amen.

Until Next Time …

- Read Chapter 23: Lies About Sex, Part 1

- Ask the Lord, "What do You want me to learn from this chapter?"

Chapter 23 Guide

Lies About Sex, Part 1

Recap

- Your sexuality comes from God and reflects His glory.

- Gender identity and biological sex are the same thing.

- Sexual shame came after the fall and comes from the devil; he wants to make sure you never accomplish God's purpose for your life.

- It is your job as the parent to teach your children about sex and sexuality.

  o Don't let them learn from the internet.

  o When they come to you with tough questions, it's okay to step back and think about what you're going to say.

  o Answer their questions honestly and in an age-appropriate way.

The Big Idea

The sex educator of today's society is Satan. Let's fight to take back that arena! And it begins by becoming aware of the lies the enemy wants to teach our children.

Chapter Review

Let's examine the most common lies the enemy tells us and our children about sex.

Lie #1: Only vaginal intercourse counts as "sex."

In God's eyes, sex is not exclusively physical. Jesus said that even looking at someone lustfully is committing adultery (Matthew 5:28). Our bodies are the temple of the Holy Spirit (1 Corinthians 6:19). The Temple in Israel had four parts: the outer court, the inner court, the Holy Place, and the Holy of Holies. Our outer court is our hands and forearms, which we use to greet anyone. Our inner court is the chest, back, and face—a stranger shouldn't touch these, but a close friend or relative can. Our Holy Place is the bottom and lips—you may only kiss a few people, and very few people should have access to your bottom. Our Holy of Holies is the genitals—only one person can go there, and that's your spouse. To touch those areas is to have sex.

Lie #2: Sex is the best way to express love.

There are plenty of people who only want to get something from you. That is not love. Neither is infatuation or "puppy love." And love certainly never demands something. Love is expressed through the commitment of marriage, the joining of two people's lives together in the presence of God. If your child is dating, maybe they've found "the one." But more likely, they're dating someone else's future wife or husband. Either way, they need to treat them with respect and honor. A boyfriend or girlfriend is not like a car to be used and then traded in for a newer model.

Lie #3: Experience makes you a better lover.

You do not have to be sexually experienced in order to satisfy your spouse in marriage. In fact, the most sexually satisfied people in marriage are the least sexual before they get married. On the other hand, people who had a lot of sex before marriage often have a fear of intimacy and may have sub-par relationship skills.

Lie #4: Sex deepens your intimacy before marriage.

Sex does not help you determine if you and your partner are really meant for each other. Sex and cohabitation before marriage only prolong an unhealthy relationship. Women tend to cohabitate before marriage because they want to keep the man from leaving. Men tend to cohabitate before marriage because they can have the conveniences of marriage, including sex, without the commitment. Couples who cohabitate before marriage have a higher divorce rate than people who do not.

The covenant of marriage is the act of giving away your rights and serving and committing to another person for the rest of your life until death. Cohabitation and a focus on sex devalue the other person.

The purpose of dating is to see how good your character is and to make sure you are *spiritually* compatible. Through dating, you get a glimpse at how deep your partner's relationship with God really is, though sometimes outside eyes are needed. But if both you and your partner are sold out for Jesus, and you know and love each other, then sex will be phenomenal once you get married.

Lie #5: Pornography doesn't hurt anyone.

Pornography is more readily accessible than ever with the technology currently available. It's not just a boy issue. And it's not just about nakedness, beautiful men and women, or sex. Until we realize what pornography is really about and attack the thought system behind it, we will never be free.

The people in pornography are explicitly presented as objects that are marketable and tailored to the partaker's "needs." As such, frequent porn consumers are more likely to sexually objectify and dehumanize others, and are more likely to commit sexual assault or allow it to happen.

Lie #6: Parents shouldn't talk to their kids about masturbation.

Masturbation is when someone stimulates or manipulates their own genitals, usually for self-pleasure, but it can also refer to non-intercourse activity with a partner. As with pornography, ignoring this topic will not make it go away.

But what should our response be to masturbation? First, we must be honest with our kids without shaming them and without feeling shame ourselves. God designed our bodies to feel pleasure when our genitals are stimulated.

We must never give our children the impression that God gave them sinful bodies. Feeling sexual pleasure is not inherently wrong. On the other hand, as children of God, we shouldn't be a slave to anything, including our sexual desires. If masturbation leads to addiction of any kind, it should be avoided. At the same time, many children don't discover masturbation through lust. Their body simply experiences a spontaneous sensation. For boys this usually happens while sleeping, which is called a "wet dream." It is natural and involuntary. And it is nothing to be ashamed of.

If you shame your children about sexuality when they are young, they will grow up and bring that shame into their sexual relationship with their spouse. Our children should never feel they have to hide anything from us. The topic of masturbation is uncomfortable, even scary. And know that it's normal for a parent to be mortified when their kids do sexual things. (We promise that your kids feel the same way about you!) If the idea of having this conversation bothers you, spend time with the Lord and bring your discomfort to Him. If there is something you are ashamed of, ask Him to forgive you. He is faithful to forgive, set you free from past burdens, *and* give you wisdom when talking with your child.

Scripture Reading

Or do you not know that your body is the temple of the Holy Spirit *who is* in you, whom you have from God, and you are not your own (1 Corinthians 6:19)?

For He Himself has said, "I will never leave you nor forsake you" (Hebrews 13:5).

Flee sexual immorality. Every sin that a man does is outside the body, but he who commits sexual immorality sins against his own body (1 Corinthians 6:18).

Discussion Questions

1. How can parents teach their children that sex is a sacred gift from God meant only for marriage?

2. How should unmarried Christian couples set appropriate physical boundaries in their relationships?

3. How can Christians develop a healthy, biblical view of sex? How can we get over an unhealthy aversion to the topic while respecting its sacredness?

Reflection Questions

1. How has the mainstream view of sex influenced your own values and behaviors regarding sexuality?

2. Have you ever compromised your values or boundaries regarding sex or intimacy? What did you learn from that experience?

3. What boundaries can you instruct and encourage your children to use when they date?

Connect with the Father

Dear Father, give me wisdom about sex and sexuality. Forgive me for the times when I misunderstood its importance. Help me to train up my children against the lies of the enemy. Help me to always be honest with them so that they can understand this gift that You have given us. In Jesus' name, Amen.

Until Next Time …

- Read Chapter 24: Lies About Sex, Part 2
- Ask the Lord, "What do You want me to learn from this chapter?"

Lies About Sex, Part 2

Recap

- Some lies that the enemy tells about sex include:

  o Only vaginal intercourse counts as "sex."
  o Sex is the best way to express love.
  o Experience makes you a better lover.
  o Sex deepens your intimacy before marriage.
  o Pornography doesn't hurt anyone.
  o Parents shouldn't talk to their kids about masturbation.

The Big Idea

God is a loving Father who cares deeply for His children. Only by staying within His boundaries can we experience true and lasting pleasure in sexual intimacy.

Chapter Review

Lie #7: Sex without rules is more fun.

Many people believe that unrestrained sex outside of marriage with no biblical morality to hinder them is the most fulfilling and exciting kind of intimacy. Yet studies have shown the exact opposite. Religion and spirituality have a strong association with sex-life satisfaction.

One of the reasons sex is better in marriage is because there is no risk of disease. There is not one disease that is spread by monogamous heterosexual sex. Sexually transmitted diseases (STDs) begin as sexually transmitted infections (STIs) and are only considered a "disease" when symptoms appear. The long-term complications of STDs include pelvic inflammatory disease, infertility, cancer, severe birth defects, and even death. Having sex outside of marriage increases your risk of getting an STI/STD and inhibits your sexual freedom.

Another reason sex is better in marriage is the trust that is built from a lifetime commitment. In marriage, you are having sex with someone who has completely devoted themselves to you in spite of your flaws and problems.

Lie #8: God isn't a fan of sex.

It is true that God put boundaries on sex. But He put those in place for our protection and enjoyment. He designed sex for both pleasure and procreation of the human race. Unfortunately, sex has also been one of the most exploited of all our sinful weaknesses.

To understand the nature of sexual intimacy, we must understand the nature of God. He wanted us to have pleasure and a relationship bonded in intimacy and mutual satisfaction. He put rules in place to protect that pleasure from destruction. Rules are not meant to be a burden but a producer of joy.

For our protection, God forbids these sexual practices:

1. Sex outside of marriage.

2. Sexual relations with a member of the same sex.

3. Sexual relations with a member of your family.

4. Sexual relations with minors.

5. Sexual relations with animals.

6. Sexual fantasies or desires for someone other than your spouse.

God is not a prude, and sex is not dirty. By trusting God and accepting His restrictions, we actually find sexual fun and fulfillment.

Lie #9: The Bible isn't fair.

It's commonly believed that the Bible's standards for sex are unfair because some people are "born a certain way," and its restrictions create prejudice against these people. Now, we are all born with a sin nature with a disposition for various sins, but in 1 Corinthians 6:9–10, Paul lists those who are unrighteous and will not inherit the kingdom of God. This list includes homosexuals and sodomites. In this passage, "homosexual" refers to the person on the giving end of the homosexual act, while "sodomite" refers to the one on the receiving end. But these are not the only sexual sins, and they are not the "worst," because all sexual sins are the same before God.

There is a difference between committing sin and practicing sin. Committing sin means you do it, but you repent and never want to do it again. Practicing sin is a lifestyle choice that you don't intend to stop. All of us commit sin from time to time, which is why we need God's mercy and grace. Practicing sin is when we get into trouble.

People will use the word "love" to validate their unhindered sexual behavior. Or they will point to the pleasure that sexuality brings as their justification. This "sex-positivity" movement teaches our children that no one should be able to tell them what to do with their own bodies. It tells them that the most important part of their identity is their sexuality. As parents, we must teach our children about Jesus, because only in Him do we find our identity. Satan wants us to find our identity in anything (and everything) else. By doing that, we surrender to our desires and give them more power over our lives than the truth of Scripture.

Obviously, the Bible is not "sex-positive," and neither is God. Those people who say they can't help themselves are telling the truth—*they* can't help themselves, Only Jesus can. That's why we need Him. And He is willing to help.

One argument that is typically used is that homosexuality is not actually a sin because Jesus never said anything about it. But with that logic, pedophilia and bestiality must not be sins either because Jesus never explicitly condemned them. But Jesus didn't have to condemn homosexuality because the Jews of His day knew that it was contrary to the Mosaic Law (Leviticus 18:22; 20:13). The Bible must be taken in its full context at all times.

Hate isn't the answer for those who are practicing sexual sin. If we condemn homosexuality, we must condemn adultery too. They are the same to God. When the Pharisees brought a woman caught in adultery to Jesus, His response was, "He who is without sin among you, let him throw a stone at her first" (John 8:7). No one could throw a stone. And Jesus did not. He did not condemn her, but He also did not condone her sin. He told her to "go and sin no more" (John 8:11). God does not condone sin, but neither is He hateful or spiteful. He is merciful and wants everyone to receive His love.

Scripture Reading

The husband should fulfill his marital duty to his wife, and likewise the wife to her husband. The wife does not have authority over her own body but yields it to her husband. In the same way, the husband does not have authority over his own body but yields it to his wife (1 Corinthians 7:3–4 NIV).

Therefore a man shall leave his father and mother and be joined to his wife, and they shall become one flesh (Genesis 2:24).

Do you not know that the unrighteous will not inherit the kingdom of God? Do not be deceived. Neither fornicators, nor idolaters, nor adulterers, nor homosexuals, nor sodomites, nor thieves, nor covetous, nor drunkards, nor revilers, nor extortioners will inherit the kingdom of God (1 Corinthians 6:9–10).

Discussion Questions

1. How does sex within marriage build trust and intimacy between spouses? Why does this matter for sexual satisfaction?

2. Is it valid to claim homosexuality is not a sin since Jesus never directly condemned it? Why or why not?

3. How did Jesus treat the woman caught in adultery? What lesson does this teach us?

Reflection Questions

1. How has culture shaped your view of sex? How has the Bible shaped your view of sex?

2. How can you have productive conversations with your children when they come to you with questions about sex?

3. Are there some sexual sins that you see as worse than others? How can you show love to those who practice them without condoning or condemning them?

Connect with the Father

Dear Father, thank You for Your love and Your Word. Thank You that because You have forgiven me, I can forgive others and show them love. Help me to have meaningful conversations with my children about the truth of Your Word. Help me to show them that You want what's best for them and that You don't want to deprive them of pleasure. In Jesus' name, Amen.

Until Next Time …

- Read Chapter 25: The Power of Biblical Meditation

- Ask the Lord, "What do You want me to learn from this chapter?"

Chapter 25 Guide

The Power of Biblical Meditation

Recap

- Other lies the enemy tells our children about sexuality:

    o Sex without rules is more fun.
    o God isn't a fan of sex.
    o The Bible isn't fair.

- God has put rules in place to protect the pleasure and importance of sex.

- God is not hateful, and He does not want to deprive us of what is good.

The Big Idea

The many dangers children face is daunting. The weapon of our warfare must be constant meditation on the Word of God!

Chapter Review

Parenting is often more challenging than we thought it would be. There always seem to be new things to fear and new challenges to face, both for the parents and for the children. The key to overcoming these challenges is biblical meditation.

"Meditation" here is not the New Age meditation where you empty your mind and try to become one with the universe. Biblical meditation means to rehearse Scripture in your mind and out loud so that its truth becomes hidden in your heart.

Your strongest weapon is the Sword of the Spirit, which is the Word of God (Ephesians 6:17). The enemy is no match for it. No amount of self-help or groveling before God in shame will bring the victory that truly *knowing* Scripture brings. This sort of knowing is more than just head knowledge. It stirs up faith within you to be able to believe that God is faithful and loving. Biblical meditation does not mean you will never be tempted again, but you will be able to overcome that temptation.

To meditate is like "ruminating," or chewing cud. When a sheep chews cud, it chews, swallows, and then regurgitates to chew again. The cud passes through multiple stomachs that refine it until it can be digested in a pure form. Biblical meditation is taking a Bible verse, chapter, or story and bringing it back to your mind throughout the day to mentally "chew" on it.

You might think you're too busy during the day to meditate on the Word. But simply bringing it to mind while you're driving, cooking, or eating lunch will sow the Word into your heart and help you enjoy the presence and power of God. Your heavenly Father wants to be a part of every moment of your life, and His presence inhabits His Word. Biblical meditation is a great way to give your time to Him, even in the midst of life. So is singing praises to Him from your heart and singing songs that focus on His Word. The enemy doesn't take breaks during the day from tempting you or attacking your thought life, so it's best to have your sword in your hand at all times.

God designed every area of your life to operate according to His Word. His love and His Word empower us to live as He wants us to live and to believe what He wants us to believe. If you feel like God doesn't love you, then meditate on Scriptures about God's love. If you're struggling with fear, meditate on Scriptures about how God is your faithful protector. The more you meditate on Scripture, the more you will remember it when you need it most.

God promises that when we meditate on His Word "day and night," everything we do will prosper. When our minds are filled with the Word of God, the attacks of the enemy that come when we're watching TV, listening to music, or just lying in bed silently won't stick. There's no place for them because your mind is occupied with the truth.

The idea of meditating on Scripture scares some people away because they think that they aren't "spiritual enough" or that it's too difficult. But any man, woman, or child can meditate on Scripture day and night. Even focusing on just one verse that stuck out to you during your morning reading will profit your soul and defend your mind. The enemy will attack you whether you feel "spiritual" or not. You can't stop his attacks from coming. In other words, you can't take thoughts out of your mind or prevent them from coming in. But you *can* fill your mind with the right thoughts! A depressive or suicidal thought might enter your mind without your consent, but you don't have to claim it as your own, and you don't have to dwell on it. You just need to replace it with the greater truth of God's Word.

As parents, we must use this weapon for ourselves and for our families, and we must train our children to wield the Word of God for themselves. The Word of God is greater than any weapon of the enemy. It is the power of God that works in us when we believe it and confess it. Whatever you or your children are going through, the Word of God will set you free.

Scripture Reading

That which has been *is* what will be,
That which *is* done is what will be done,
And *there is* nothing new under the sun
(Ecclesiastes 1:9).

How can a young man cleanse his way?
By taking heed according to Your word.
With my whole heart I have sought You;
Oh, let me not wander from Your commandments!
Your word I have hidden in my heart,
That I might not sin against You (Psalm 119:9–11).

And do not be drunk with wine, in which is dissipation; but be filled with the Spirit, speaking to one another in psalms and hymns and spiritual songs, singing and making melody in your heart to the Lord (Ephesians 5:18–19).

Then they cried out to the LORD in their trouble,
And He saved them out of their distresses.
He sent His word and healed them,
And delivered *them* from their destructions
(Psalm 107:19–20).

Discussion Questions

1. How is biblical meditation different from other forms of meditation?

2. Why is it important to meditate on Scripture day and night?

3. What are some creative ways to teach children to meditate on Scripture?

Reflection Questions

1. How might biblical meditation strengthen your faith and your ability to stand firm against the enemy?

2. What struggles are you currently facing? What struggles are your children facing? What Scriptures can you meditate on to fight against those challenges?

3. How can you be more intentional about meditating on God's Word during the day?

Connect with the Father

Dear Father, Your Word is magnificent! It is a lamp to my feet and a light to my path. Teach me to love Your Word. Teach me how to meditate on it day and night. Thank You that as more and more Scripture gets into my heart, it will strengthen me against the attacks of the enemy. Show me Scriptures that will drive away any lies I might believe. Help me to teach my children. Give them a love for Your Word. In Jesus' name, Amen.

Until Next Time …

- Read the Epilogue: Is It Too Late?
- Ask the Lord, "What do You want me to learn from this chapter?"

Epilogue Guide

Is It Too Late?

Recap

- The Word of God is your most powerful weapon against the attacks of the enemy that come to destroy you and your children.

- Biblical meditation is rehearsing Scripture in your mind and out loud throughout the day.

- God promises that when we meditate on Scripture He will make everything we do prosper.

The Big Idea

Never lose hope for your child even if they stray.
Stay in prayer and keep the faith. It's never too late
for your child to accept Christ.

Chapter Review

It is easy to become disheartened when your children still seem lost or have gone astray. It can feel
as though you failed. But hear us: *It is not your
fault*. We all make mistakes as parents. None of
us are perfect. If you made mistakes that had poor
effects on your kids but have repented for those
mistakes, ask for forgiveness from your children
and do what you can to make it right. You cannot
change the past, but you can decide not to repeat it.

No matter if your mistakes were big or small,
your children were created with a free will. They
have the choice to either serve God or not serve
Him. You can't make the choice for them, and you
can't take responsibility for what they choose.

Maybe it feels as though you've lost the fight. But
don't lose hope! Keep praying for your children. As
E. M. Bounds wrote, "Prayers live before God, and
God's heart is set on them, and [so] prayers outlive
the lives who uttered them." Naturally, you want to
see your children follow God. But even if *you* don't
see it happen, it can still happen! Maybe they won't
decide to follow Jesus while you're still living, but

as long as there is still breath in *their* lungs, it isn't too late.

Don't give up. Keep praying. Keep fighting for the soul of your child.

Scripture Reading

Therefore take up the whole armor of God, that you may be able to withstand in the evil day, and having done all, to stand (Ephesians 6:13).

The soul who sins shall die. The son shall not bear the guilt of the father, nor the father bear the guilt of the son. The righteousness of the righteous shall be upon himself, and the wickedness of the wicked shall be upon himself (Ezekiel 18:20).

Now faith is the substance of things hoped for, and the evidence of things not seen (Hebrews 11:1).

Discussion Questions

1. How does the statement "You can't make the choice for your child, and ultimately, you can't take responsibility for their choice" bring comfort to a parent?

2. Why do you think Christian parents tend to be so hard on themselves when their kids rebel or stray?

3. How does prayer have the power to impact future generations?

Reflection Questions

1. Are there any mistakes you have made that you feel ashamed about? How can you move past the shame?

2. How can you stay encouraged when your children seem to be straying from God?

3. Reflect on a time when you experience God's faithfulness in a situation that seemed hopeless. How can remembering past miracles increase your faith for present prayers?

Connect with the Father

Dear Father, I'm not giving up! I'm not throwing in the towel. Give me the strength to continue fighting for the soul of my child. Help me to put everything I have learned into practice. Guide my decisions and give me wisdom. Be with my children and make them Yours. Give me patience as they make their own choices and mistakes. Help me to love them like You love them. Bless them and give them Your peace. In Jesus' name, Amen.

Thank You

As a family, we thank you for your dedication and commitment to fighting for the soul of your child. You have taken a vital step in equipping yourself with the biblical wisdom and practical tools needed to navigate the challenges of godly parenting in today's world.

Remember, you are not alone in this battle. God chose you to be your child's parent, and He will provide you with the strength, courage, and guidance you need. Continue to seek Him through prayer as you daily meditate on His Word and trust in His unending faithfulness.

As you apply the principles you have learned, be encouraged that your efforts are multiplied by the power of the Holy Spirit, and they will have a lasting impact on your child's life as well as future generations. Never give up hope, even in the face of adversity. Keep fighting the good fight, knowing that your partnership with the Lord is not in vain.

May God bless you and your family!

Jimmy, Karen, and Julie

Notes

Chapter 1 Guide—The Greater Purpose

1. "Proverbs 22," *Pulpit Commentary* on Bible Hub, accessed May 30, 2023, https://biblehub.com/commentaries /pulpit/proverbs/22.htm.

Chapter 3 Guide—The Soul War

1. "5315. Nephesh," Bible Hub, https://biblehub.com /hebrew/5315.htm.

2. "Psuché," *Thayer's Greek Lexicon* on Bible Hub, https://biblehub.com/thayers/5590.htm.

Chapter 4 Guide—Dressed to Kill

1. "222. Alétheia," Bible Hub, https://biblehub.com /greek/225.htm.

2. "3162. Macharira," Bible Hub, https://biblehub.com /greek/3162.htm.

Chapter 6 Guide—Missile Launch

1. "Forgiveness: Your Health Depends on It," Johns Hopkins Medicine, November 1, 2021, https://www .hopkinsmedicine.org/health/wellness-and-prevention /forgiveness-your-health-depends-on-it.

Chapter 9 Guide—A Biblical Worldview

1. George Barna, "American Worldview Inventory 2023 Release #1: Incidence of Biblical Worldview Shows Significant Change Since the Start of the Pandemic," February 28, 2023, Cultural Research Center, https://www .arizonachristian.edu/wp-content/uploads/2023/02/CRC _AWVI2023_Release1.pdf.

2. George Barna, "American Worldview Inventory 2022 Release #4: Improving Parents' Ability to Raise Spiritual Champions," April 22, 2022, Cultural Research Center, https://www.arizonachristian.edu/wp-content /uploads/2022/04/AWVI2022_Release_04_Digital.pdf.

www.ingramcontent.com/pod-product-compliance
Lightning Source LLC
LaVergne TN
LVHW051402080426
835508LV00022B/2932